Los Lobos

AMERICAN MUSIC SERIES

Peter Blackstock and David Menconi, Editors

DREAM IN BLUE

~~~~~~

BY CHRIS MORRIS

UNIVERSITY OF TEXAS PRESS

AUSTIN

Requests for permission to reproduce material from
this work should be sent to:
    Permissions
    University of Texas Press
    P.O. Box 7819
    Austin, TX 78713-7819
    http://utpress.utexas.edu/index.php/rp-form

♾ The paper used in this book meets the minimum
requirements of ANSI/NISO Z39.48-1992 (R1997)
(Permanence of Paper).

Library of Congress Cataloging-in-Publication Data

Morris, Chris (Music journalist), author.
Los Lobos : dream in blue / by Chris Morris.
    pages   cm — (American music series)
    Includes bibliographical references.
    ISBN 978-0-292-74823-1 (cloth : alkaline paper)
    ISBN 978-1-4773-0853-0 (library e-book)
    ISBN 978-1-4773-0852-3 (nonlibrary e-book)
1. Lobos (Musical group) 2. Rock groups—
California—East Los Angeles. I. Title. II. Series:
American music series (Austin, Tex.)
    ML421.L65M67   2015
    782.42164092′2—dc23   2015004314

doi: 10.7560/748231

For my sons,
Max and Zane

CONTENTS

PROLOGUE
Cinco de Mayo

In 2012, Los Lobos were granted their own festival in Los Angeles. Under the auspices of the Nederlander Organization, the national concert venue and promotion firm, the East L.A. band mounted their first daylong event at the Greek Theatre, a spacious, verdant amphitheater carved out of a hillside above the city's Los Feliz neighborhood, many miles from L.A.'s East Side, where the band was born and bred.

It was the natural location for the show. The Lobos had enjoyed a history with the Greek dating back to July 1985, when the band—yet to make a big national mark, but already a much-loved local institution—made the first of several summertime appearances there. These events were among the most unforgettable concerts of the mid-'80s. East L.A. homeboys and homegirls poured into the Greek in their finery, rubbing elbows with locals from the rock scene who had witnessed Los Lobos' swift rise through the ranks of the Hollywood roots–punk axis. It was the biggest party in town.

"We've always had a pretty special relationship with the Greek," Steve Berlin, the band's saxophonist–keyboardist, told me the week before the first festival. "They were very kind to us over the years, and we've had some pretty special nights there."

Appropriately, the 2012 Los Lobos Festival was presented on Cinco de Mayo, the Mexican national holiday celebrating the country's improbable victory over invading French forces at the Battle of Puebla on that date in 1862. The event at the Greek dovetailed naturally with the customary citywide *fiesta* thrown by L.A.'s enormous Mexican American population.

The inaugural 2012 festival, staged under crystalline skies on a summer day, was very much a family affair. In the afternoon, on the terrace outside the amphitheater, the acts playing on a small jury-rigged stage included the 44s, a bluesy rock unit that included drummer Jason Lozano, son of Los Lobos' bassist Conrad Lozano, and David "Kid" Ramos, formerly guitarist for the Fabulous Thunderbirds; Ollin, a folk–punk act that served as the house band for *Evangeline, the Queen of Make-Believe*, a local multimedia show based on the Lobos songbook that premiered a week later; and La Santa Cecilia, a young East L.A. group that drew heavily on the Lobos' original folk model. (The latter act would break through to wider recognition with their first full-length studio album, *Treinta Dias*, which won a Grammy Award in 2014 for Best Latin Rock, Urban, or Alternative Album.)

It was old home week on the main stage as well. The crowd was warmed up by Mariachi El Bronx, a brawny unit fusing traditional *mariachi* (the Mexican string and horn ensemble style) and punk rock, which included *bajo sexto* player Vince Hidalgo, son of Lobos guitarist David Hidalgo, among their colorfully costumed members, and X, the legendary punk band with whom the Lobos had shared bills in their earliest days in Hollywood.

When Los Lobos came out of the wings in the gloaming to robust cheers, they arrayed themselves before the crowd in their traditional onstage positions. To the audience's far left stood Cesar Rosas, the band's southpaw singer–guitarist, still the eminent Chicano hipster, his eyes masked by omnipresent Ray-Bans, a neat goatee on his chin; he remains the taciturn group's default master of ceremonies, and introduced most of the songs with a quip or an exclamation, acknowledging applause with "*Gracias* very much." To Rosas's left shoulder was Conrad Lozano, the most animated of the players, who bounced on the balls of his feet as he plucked his bass or monstrous *guitarron*, grinning broadly. Formerly seated atop the drum chair to the rear (now occupied by the boyish touring drummer Enrique "Bugs" Gonzalez), the small, almost doll-like Louie Pérez now commanded center stage, playing guitar and, on the traditional numbers that invariably grace the group's set, a variety of acoustic stringed instruments. Next to him was his broad, moon-faced songwriting partner David Hidalgo; ever a retiring and almost bashful figure, he kept his onstage patter to the barest minimum, content to dazzle the audience with his soaring vocals and his virtuosity on guitar, accordion, and an arsenal of stringed instruments. Finally, Steve Berlin stood behind an electronic keyboard at the audience's right, his battery of reed and wind instruments on stands behind him; "the new kid," the Jewish saxophonist from Philly who joined Los Lobos in 1983, is so perfectly assimilated into the group that he might now be mistaken for an East Side homie, with his head crowned with a felt cap, eyes covered like Cesar's with dark glasses, a long, pointed beard on his chin.

Old friends and fans joined the main attraction during their headlining stint, which commenced with an acoustic mini-set. Titian-haired Americana goddess Neko Case dueted with David Hidalgo on "One Time One Night." Another Americana icon, the Texas-based Chicano singer–songwriter Alejandro Escovedo, fronted the group on his compositions "Rosalie" and "Rebel Kind," a staple for his '80s band the True Believers, road mates of Los Lobos in their first days of touring. Accordionist Flaco Jimenez—the seventy-three-year-old star of *norteño* (Tex–Mex border) music and David Hidalgo's principal inspiration on the instrument—and guitarist Max Baca of the contemporary border music combo (or *conjunto*) Los Texmaniacs backed Cesar Rosas on the hip-grinding Latin *bolero* (ballad) "Volver, Volver." Singer–songwriter–guitarist Dave Alvin, whose group the Blasters had introduced the Lobos to L.A. punkdom, performed his composition "4th of July," a number he had first recorded as a member of X, with Jimenez behind him. Dave remained onstage to back his brother Phil on a rocking version of the Blasters' neo-rockabilly classic "Marie Marie"—sung in Spanish, of course, as "Maria, Maria"—that filled the aisles with dancing fans.

As ever, it was a straight-ahead performance by the stars of the show. The enduring elements of a Los Lobos show are its lack of crowd-pandering or superfluous flash, and its fundamental gravity. Save for Rosas's ad-libs and the occasional interjection by the ever-reticent Hidalgo, the coolly undemonstrative group has always left it to their considerable musicianship—especially to Hidalgo's multi-instrumental virtuosity and Rosas's fret firepower—to carry the show. In ways both visual and musical, they resemble a group of '60s-era elders with whom they shared stages in the 1980s: the Grateful Dead. A Los Lobos performance is invariably fun, but there is simultaneously never any doubt that the band members are *serious* about what they do. And so it was at the Greek.

The first Lobos Cinco de Mayo Fest proved so successful that it was repeated a year to the day later with a different cast of supporting acts. The previous year's sunshine was in short supply. The date took place under uncommonly gray L.A. skies; an intermittent drizzle dampened the festivities and sent some audience members heading for the exits early during the latter part of the night. La Santa Cecilia returned for the afternoon portion of the show, joined by Los Fabulocos (Kid Ramos's band) and Making Movies, a bilingual Latino–roots act from Kansas City with an album produced by Steve Berlin to their credit.

Unlike the previous year, there was no punk act in the lineup to enlist the graying rockers, and the 2013 festival drew a higher percentage of Latinos among its audience members. The opening acts on the big stage were El Chicano, the '70s band from East L.A. that scored huge hits with the *bolero* "Sabor a Mi" (part of the Lobos' early repertoire) and the instrumental "Viva Tirado"; Kinky, the in-your-face, techno-flavored *rock en Español* group from Monterrey, Mexico; and Pedro Torres y Su Mariachi, a local act playing in the traditional *mariachi* style.

Beyond the presence of the gospel-reared steel guitarist Robert Randolph—who capped the night with duels on Jimi Hendrix's "Purple Haze," Ritchie Valens's "Come On, Let's Go," and the Lobos' "Mas y Mas"—guests for the headliners' set were similarly Latin in flavor. A couple of highlights were contributed by members of Los Super Seven, the Tex–Mex supergroup that numbered the Lobos among their personnel on their first two albums: Ruben Ramos tore up the *bolero* "Paloma Negra," while Rick Treviño honored George Jones, who had died the previous month, with a moving cover of the country singer's "He Stopped Loving Her Today." Members of Kinky brought their electronic style to a collaborative rendering of "Kiko and the Lavender Moon." Returnee Max Baca (also a charter member of Los Super Seven) and his nephew, accordionist Josh Baca, stepped in for "Margarita." And Little Willie G., lead vocalist of the '60s East L.A. rock act Thee Midniters, fronted the group for three numbers, climaxing with his old band's ballad hit "That's All."

~~~~~~

The two Cinco de Mayo Festivals—which were succeeded in 2014 with a third holiday event, with the popular local Latino rock act Ozomatli in support—were more than a demonstration of Los Lobos' totemic position in L.A.'s musical firmament. The band's prominence—perhaps most notably acknowledged by three Grammy Awards and a 2014 Lifetime Achievement Award from the Latin Grammys—had long ago transcended local-hero status. On October 13, 2009, they had appeared before President Barack Obama as part of Fiesta Latina, a celebration of Latino American music on the White House lawn. During the televised event, the president could be seen singing along to "La Bamba," the song that had thrown the group into the national spotlight in 1987, when their cover of the Ritchie Valens number became a No. 1 hit.

The Greek Theatre shows significantly dramatized the breadth of Los Lobos' audience. Put in the terms of their hometown's cultural and demographic map, it's as much West Side as East Side. Over time, they became cherished by white, middle-class rock fans who had been drawn to the band's seamless mating of Latin and American roots styles, and who had stayed on board as they incorporated increasingly innovative textures into their music. But the band has never lost touch with the neighborhood—the *barrio* fans who had embraced them in the early '70s as they became the first young group in East Los Angeles to explore the traditional music of Mexico and Latin America. The ranks from both camps swelled during the course of their career to encompass three discreet groups of listeners—O.G. East Siders who had slow-danced to "Sabor a Mi" at backyard parties in Montebello; old punks who had rocked out to "Don't Worry Baby" at Club Lingerie; and their children and grandchildren who had been captivated by "La Bamba" on the radio or pulled the old LPs and CDs off the family shelf.

The Cinco de Mayo concerts also cumulatively charted the remarkable progress of Los Lobos' music, which over the course of time has come to encompass as many stylistic streams as that of such famous precursors and Rock and Roll Hall of Famers as Creedence Clearwater Revival, the Band, the Grateful Dead, and ZZ Top (the latter of whom is the only major American act presently at work that rivals them in terms of longevity, on a continuous basis). Few groups in rock history have demonstrated such expansive reach or creative restlessness.

Many will refer to Los Lobos as a "Chicano" band, but it is in the (today) lesser-used term "Mexican American" that the truest sources of their art may be defined. Though all four of the band's original core members of the '70s are of Mexican descent, three of them were born in Los Angeles and were raised in predominantly English-speaking households, and all of them grew up listening to and ultimately playing in American roots styles. They essentially taught themselves the music of their Hispanic forebears when they formed their original folk music incarnation, Los Lobos del Este de Los Angeles, in the early '70s, during the height of the Chicano renaissance in the city. However, in the '80s, they melded those Latino roots with their early electric influences and made a name for themselves on the post-punk roots–rock scene of Hollywood.

Achieving international fame with the retro commercial triumph of "La Bamba," they stepped back and—after re-exploring their Mexican American folk roots on a Grammy-winning album—they once again reconfigured their sound with a series of exploratory, sometimes wildly experimental recordings during the 1990s that are among the most boundary-pushing works formulated by an American band of the era. After the turn of the millennium, their albums found the Lobos steeping in a now-organic blend of all these styles. They had by then truly returned to their roots, writing and recording their albums independently after decades of work in the U.S. major-label sphere.

Over the course of their four decades together, Los Lobos ranged through virtually the entire breadth of American vernacular music, seamlessly integrating a plethora of influences in their sui generis sound. Certainly, they were and are at heart a rock 'n' roll band, but the term in their case spans the history of the music, from rockabilly through sophisticated '60s rock into primal punk rock. But the music explored all the other major American genre tributaries—blues, R&B and soul, country, folk. Their take on Latin music, the original source of their sound, was similarly catholic in orientation, moving from the *son jarocho* of Mexico—a song style of the Veracruz region from which the group drew heavily—to the accordion-driven sound of the Texas–Mexico border *conjuntos* (small bands) to, later, the swaying *cumbia* of Colombia and Panama. During the '90s, at the height of their creative powers, they further upped the ante by injecting all the components of their work with a fresh experimental rigor, chopping and channeling the music like an East Side mechanic at work on a lowrider.

Each distinct new chapter in Los Lobos' musical development arrived organically, essentially as a procession of responses to a series of challenges. Though they were rock musicians in their formative teen years, their first manifestation as a Mexican American folk group amid the flourishing of the '60s Chicano rebirth grew out of a desire to probe the roots of their native culture, which had grown remote to them and to others in their hometown community through the process of assimilation. Later, after their folk music met with an initially violent reaction from the nascent L.A. punk rock community, they took that hostility as a thrown gauntlet and, picking up their electric instruments again, they entered the local rock scene with born-again fervor. After conquering that scene, and ultimately the American record charts, with their roots–punk style, they reclaimed their folk origins. After hitting a creative wall amid the snares of rock stardom, they forged into terra incognita with a series of boldly label-defying recordings that reflected the influence of rock's most avant-garde practitioners. Their mature style reconciled the many strains and strands of their music.

The sheer length of their reach and the breadth of their sound summon up a long list of questions about Los Lobos' identity. Their polarities are many. Are they Mexican or American? Hippies or punks? Folk artists or rockers? Traditionalists or experimentalists? Conservatives or radicals? At the end of the day, the answer must surely be "All of the above." It is the very complexity of Los Lobos' music, and their unwillingness to be constrained by the world's notions of what they ought to be, that has sustained the band as a creative unit for forty years, and that makes them such an extraordinary and incomparable force in this country's music.

In the course of charting Los Lobos' story, I contacted Tom Waits, a Los Angeles–bred artist of similar artistic orientation, and one who likewise has taken traditional music to the most outré frontiers of popular style. Like the best and most imaginative of Los Lobos' music, his seems to exist in a kind of rarefied dream state.

Waits had recorded a song with the Lobos, "Kitate," which appeared on the band's 2004 album *The Ride*. I was curious about his experience working with them, and passed some questions along through his publicist. Being Tom Waits, he chose to respond with his own impression of the band's music. It seemed to hit the sweet spot. It read in part:

> I would love one day to sing "La Golondrina" with them. Or "Guadalajara Nunano" or "Alla En El Rancho Grande" or "Volver." They have so much range. You can trace their influences like the rings of a tree. They are Traditionalists, Cubists, Dadaists, Surrealists, and muralists. They all have chops and range and surprise and a profound depth of vernacular flavor and accent.

Listening to Los Lobos I hear fossils and fragments of pottery. One moment they are barefoot on a dirt floor and I hear babies crying. Next they are Link Wray, Howlin' Wolf, Fred McDowell distortion box. They abracadabra the world. They are the master chefs creating new cuisine. It sounds sometimes like they are trying to recreate the sounds they heard in all the rooms they ever lived in.

Los Lobos are best played loud at a carnival in a vacant lot with generators moaning like tractors and bells from game booths ringing. They are consummate musicians and you can be nourished by listening and learning. They are not "like" anything, they are Los Lobos. It's hard to drive around Los Angeles and not think of them.

What follows is a critical history of Los Lobos' musical journey. It should not be considered biographical; the focus is on the musical progress of the band, as defined principally in their recording career. Biographical details about the group's members are restricted to information that has some bearing on their creative work. It may be worth noting here that all of the musicians are family men of long standing (though Cesar Rosas lost his wife of seventeen years in 1999), and all are fathers.

The band's story will be told here primarily through their own words, though several key collaborators were also interviewed. I myself have been following that story as a journalist and a fan since 1980, and I would not have undertaken the writing of this project without a long-standing admiration for their music; I have allowed myself to enter the narrative at a couple of key junctures.

I first heard Los Lobos' music in the Hollywood clubs, where they began to attain their renown in the early '80s. But their music had its genesis years earlier, in a corner of Los Angeles that was obscure and even exotic to some. It is on that compass point that we must begin.

Los Lobos

- 1 -

THE NEIGHBORHOOD

Life and Music in East L.A.

Dave Alvin, the poet laureate of Los Angeles roots music, grew up in Downey, a largely white, working-class community notable to most music fans as the home of the Carpenters, a few miles down the Golden State Freeway from East Los Angeles. He knows the turf well.

"As you should point out, it's a different world," he says.

Riding to East L.A. from Union Station on the Metro Gold Line train, that *otherness* materializes before an observer in a way it doesn't during a trip on the wide freeways. Pulling out of downtown L.A. to pass through Little Tokyo and Boyle Heights, the community directly to the west of East L.A., the skyscrapers recede, and warehouses and low-slung commercial buildings begin to dominate the terrain. Here and there next to the tracks, as you pass through residential areas, you begin to see colorful murals celebrating Mexican and Mexican American heroes, some ablaze with Aztec imagery. After the Pico Aliso stop, the light rail line dives underground. When the train surfaces again at Soto, the world has changed. Signs in Spanish identify the businesses along the tracks. By the time you reach the terminal Atlantic Boulevard station, nearly all the other passengers on the train are Latino.

You have arrived at the heart of *La Raza* in L.A.—a seven-and-a-half-square-mile patch of unincorporated land, about five miles from downtown, bordered by Boyle Heights on the west, Monterey Park and Montebello on the east, and City of

Commerce on the south. It was here that waves of Mexican immigrants had begun to arrive in massive numbers nearly a century ago as revolution tore at their country, and here they had settled. (Mexican nationals continue to pour into the area today, and some of the earlier generations of Mexican American families have moved to other communities—La Habra, Whittier, Fullerton.)

In a friend's car, you can seek out the musical and cultural history of East L.A., that rich past that still arcs into the present. You have to know where to look, though, because many of its landmarks have disappeared and faded into memory.

Some buildings still stand, their place in the saga uncommemorated. The homely Kennedy Hall, site of dozens of '60s rock 'n' roll dances, abides on Atlantic Boulevard; its original sign has tilted like the Tower of Pisa over the years. Driving by St. Alphonsus Catholic Church a block down the road, you'd never know that its adjacent school hall, a block off the avenue, was where the revered local band Thee Midniters played their first Battle of the Bands. Drive two blocks further to Whittier Boulevard, and the site of the Golden Gate Theater is pointed out to you. The towering gingerbread venue, where Thee Midniters shot the cover of their first album, *Whittier Boulevard*, is now a CVS pharmacy.

Turn off Atlantic onto Whittier, and you're a little surprised by how narrow the boulevard is; if you know its name only from Thee Midniters' rumbling, huge-sounding 1965 instrumental hit—the theme song of every cruiser who ever rolled down the strip on a weekend night, bedeviling the local cops—it has always appeared in your imagination in widescreen, as broad as the Champs-Élysées.

The Record Inn, John Ovalle's historic store, is gone, as are most of the record shops that used to dot the boulevard, but Sounds of Music Records and Tapes is still in business at the corner of Whittier and La Verne. You make your way through the shop's narrow aisles and thumb through bins packed with vintage vinyl, pausing in front of glass cases with cast-metal replicas of lowrider cars, stopping to admire a framed, autographed photo of East L.A. star Lalo Guerrero with President Bill Clinton and Hillary Rodham Clinton.

Reaching the rear, you pause in front of the store's office, and your heart flutters a bit as you notice a sign visible above the door: a relic of the Silver Dollar Bar—the infamous local spot where Ruben Salazar, Mexican American reporter for the *Los Angeles Times*, was killed amid the violent disturbances during the Chicano Moratorium protest of the Vietnam War on August 29, 1970, slain by a tear gas grenade fired into the bar by a Los Angeles County sheriff's deputy. You learn that the site of the bar is directly across the street from the record store. It's now a storefront church, Iglesia Cristiana Inc.; a humble laminated sign on its bright blue facade bears the dates of Salazar's birth and death.

Another, more opulently appointed church is located in an old theater a couple of blocks away, past the Whittier Boulevard archway above the street. Atop the marquee of Centro de Ayuda Spiritual towers an incongruous sign identifying the venue's former owner: HUGGY BOY—Dick "Huggy Boy" Hugg, the popular L.A. disc jockey who became a key promoter of East L.A.'s rock dances of the '60s and a major sponsor of its indigenous acts. One more fabled site of rock 'n' roll dances in the day is up the boulevard a few more blocks, on Soto Street just the other side of the Boyle Heights line: Bishop Mora Salesian High School—the Catholic boys' school where Thee Midniters, whose early gigs were promoted by Huggy Boy, got their start.

Head north and back east, and some other East Side music landmarks are visible, but you have to squint to pick them out. On Cesar Chavez Avenue in Boyle Heights—formerly Brooklyn Avenue, another of the old East Side's entertainment hubs, and renamed in 1993 for the Chicano organizer—you cruise by Casa Grande, a wan-looking building with plywood covering its windows; when it was known as the Paramount Ballroom, this was a key locale for the Chicano acts of the '60s.

Finally, heading back into the heart of East L.A., you arrive at the corner of Cesar Chavez Avenue and Marianna Avenue. On the northeast corner of the intersection stands a Pizza Hut, just one of dozens of nondescript fast-foot outlets that dot the neighborhood. On this site from 1960 to 1972 stood Lalo's, the nightclub operated by its namesake, Lalo Guerrero.

~~~~~~

Known as "the Original Chicano," Arizona-born singer, guitarist, and songwriter Eduardo "Lalo" Guerrero was an all-purpose entertainer. Active from the 1930s until the turn of the millennium, he wrote in virtually every form of Latin music, and played in almost every possible style. His hits included the *ranchera* (a tradition-based rural folk song) "Canción Mexicana," the "Ballad of Davy Crockett" parody "Pancho Lopez," and his children's recordings of "Las Ardillitas," a Mexican American answer to the Chipmunks. Crucially, he was also one of the first practitioners of a style that can be identified with the title of a 1948 hit recorded by Guerrero's contemporary Don Tosti: "Pachuco Boogie."

The pachucos—the zoot-suited Mexican American hipsters who inspired the music—had first surfaced in East Los Angeles in the late '30s and early '40s, at the height of the swing era. Though a minority within a minority, the stylish 'chucos, whose dress and posture embodied a nascent form of Mexican American pride, became a target of scorn and derision in the fearmongering Anglo media of the day. They were demonized in coverage of the notorious "Sleepy Lagoon Murder" case of 1942, in which a group of young Latinos were wrongfully charged with the slaying of another young Mexican American. A year later, during the Zoot Suit Riots of 1943, flamboyantly dressed pachucos were terrorized, beaten, and stripped on the streets of downtown L.A. by Anglo civilians and rampaging servicemen stationed in Boyle Heights.

In the postwar years, despite the adversity and the waning of swing, the pachuco survived—or, as Frank Zappa would later put it somewhat sardonically, "The present-day pachuco refuses to die." A Texas-born musician who billed himself professionally as Don Tosti found an opening to exploit the culture musically. At a 1948 session for the L.A. independent label Discos

Taxco, Tosti laid down a number arranged in the manner of the swing-influenced small-band R&B style popularized earlier in the decade by Louis Jordan's Tympany Five and the King Cole Trio. Its lyrics and dialogue were delivered in the pachuco's own *caló* slang, which Tosti had grown up with in the El Paso *barrio*. "Pachuco Boogie," credited to the pseudonymous Cuarteto Don Ramon, Sr., reputedly went on to sell a million copies in the Latino community. Tosti followed up that hit with a run of similar pachuco-themed numbers—"El Tirilli" (a tribute to marijuana smokers), "Wine-O-Boogie," "Mambo Del Pachuco," and, perhaps inevitably, "Chicano Boogie."

Lalo Guerrero, a born satirist, had already spoofed the pachuco style in some of his *corridos* (story songs) recorded for Imperial Records. He now stepped into his own pachuco boogie phase, notching a hit in 1949 with the jazzy "Muy Sabroso Blues," billed to his prophetically named combo Lalo Guerrero y Sus Cinco Lobos. He followed suit with other singles in that vein—"Chicas Patas Boogie," "Los Chucos Suaves," and the notorious "Marihuana Boogie"—that were lapped up by old fans and the pachucos themselves.

The vogue for pachuco boogie was relatively brief, though it did launch Tosti as an immensely popular attraction at the Hollywood Palladium's dance shows, which attracted large Mexican American audiences. But the die was definitely cast. It may be said that pachuco boogie was the first truly Mexican American music, for it mated the culture and colloquial speech of Mexican East L.A. with the gutsy sound of black American rhythm and blues. Its echoes would be heard a decade later, when a group of young performers in East L.A. would put their own spin on R&B.

~~~~~~

"The major influence for a lot of us was the South Central scene, the rhythm and blues scene," says Little Willie G. (né Willie Garcia), lead singer of Thee Midniters. "That had more of an impact on us than Lalo."

Garcia says he had firsthand exposure to the great R&B talents who were stars in the L.A. firmament—"Johnny Otis,

Johnny Guitar Watson, Big Jay McNeely, Joe Liggins, Don Julian and the Larks, Richard Berry—I used to shine his shoes, man. Richard Berry, Don Julian, Tony Allen, and Jesse Belvin used to rehearse on 41st Place and Long Beach Avenue, at Tony Allen's grandmother's house. As a young kid, I used to sell newspapers and shine shoes, and I used to go over there to just hear them rehearse and stuff, and I'd shine their shoes while they were rehearsing."

The up-and-coming generation of musicians in East L.A. in the '60s never turned their backs on their Hispanic heritage. Garcia notes, "It was just in our DNA to do *boleros* and *corridos*, the Mexican music thing, because we wanted to please our parents. That became part of our catalog, part of our library."

Every kid on the East Side was aware that one of the three hits recorded by Ritchie Valens, the Mexican American singer–guitarist from the San Fernando Valley, before his tragic death in February 1959, was "La Bamba," an adaptation of an old Mexican folk tune. But, like his young fans, Valens had been reared on rhythm and blues. He idolized Little Richard, and his repertoire included covers of the Robins' "Framed," Larry Williams's "Bony Maronie," and Robert & Johnny's "We Belong Together," all significant hits of the late '50s.

So, when the first Chicano bands began to surface in the early '60s, it was logical that they would make rhythm and blues an important part of their rock 'n' roll formula. In the case of one band, the cross-cultural orientation was entirely natural. Eddie Davis—the ex–actor, restaurateur, and label entrepreneur who would issue many of the biggest hits to emanate from the East Side—released an R&B-soaked live LP by the Mixtures, a polyglot Oxnard group that included Chicano, Puerto Rican, white, black, and Native American members, as the first album on his Linda label in 1962.

All the 45s from Davis's Rampart Records imprint that hit the national singles chart in 1964–1965 were covers of R&B records. "Farmer John," by the San Gabriel band the Premiers, shot to No. 19 in '64; the faux-live studio recording, goosed by shrieks supplied by the members of a local girls' car club, was in its original incarnation a 1959 hit on Specialty by the R&B duo Don & Dewey. "La La La La La," which reached No. 62 the same year in a pseudo-live version by the Lincoln Heights sextet the Blendells, was unsuccessfully originated on Motown's Tamla subsidiary by Little Stevie Wonder. The Blendells also served as the backup band on what may be Rampart's best-remembered single: "Land of 1000 Dances," a No. 30 entry in 1965 by Cannibal and the Headhunters. The East L.A. vocal quartet's version of New Orleans singer Chris Kenner's 1963 number was big enough nationwide to secure them a gig as opening act for the Beatles' 1965 U.S. tour.

Before it became a national hit, "Land of 1000 Dances" created enough of a stir on the East Side that several other local bands made it part of their set. One of these groups—who actually backed Cannibal and the Headhunters in concert on occasion—grazed the *Billboard* Hot 100 at No. 67 with their own 1965 version on the Chattahoochee label. Thee Midniters would never cut anything that close to a hit again, thanks to poor national distribution, but they became the longest-lived and most popular of East L.A.'s rock 'n' roll bands of the '60s.

Made up mainly of Salesian High students, the septet began playing, under the unlikely handle of the Gentiles, at rock 'n' roll shows mounted by the school's musical director, Bill Taggart. They also began performing at local bars, sometimes with fake mustaches painted on their underage faces. They eventually graduated to shows booked by Taggart at East L.A. College.

Under the tutelage of Eddie Torres, a former social worker who sponsored the band members' car club, the Gentiles changed their moniker to Thee Midniters (in emulation of Hank Ballard's popular King Records R&B act the Midnighters). In the wake of ripples made by "Land of 1000 Dances," Torres launched Whittier Records as an outlet for the group's work. As a result, Thee Midniters would record more prolifically than any of their East Side competition, none of which managed to muster more than a single LP.

While Little Willie G.'s smooth ballad performances—great *bolero* singing, essentially—attracted swooning attention from female members of the audience, it was the muscle of Thee Midniters' horn-driven, guitar-powered, R&B-based sound that put the group over with crowds. Their sets bulged with high-watt soul covers—of Martha and the Vandellas' "Heat Wave," the Contours' "Do You Love Me," Barrett Strong's "Money," Solomon Burke's "Everybody Needs Somebody to Love." The band also wasn't shy about tearing a page from the songbooks of the bluesiest contemporary rock acts, taking on Them's "Gloria," Mitch Ryder and the Detroit Wheels' medley "Devil with a Blue Dress On/Good Golly Miss Molly," and the Rolling Stones' "Empty Heart." They were inspired enough by the Stones to work up an instrumental based on (or, one could say, purloined from) the English act's "2120 South Michigan Avenue," the title of which nodded to the street address of rock 'n' roll, blues, and R&B label Chess Records' Chicago headquarters. Thee Midniters' "Whittier Boulevard" remains the insuperable lowrider anthem to this day.

By the time Thee Midniters were approaching the end of the line in 1968–1969, the era of *Chicanismo* was gaining steam, and, with some pushing from Eddie Torres, the band that had started life emulating black R&B acts returned to their Latino musical heritage. The band's last singles included a raucous version of the 1934 *ranchera* classic "The Big Ranch," with lusty interpolations of rowdy *caló*; a lush reading, with strings, of the *bolero* "Tu Despedida"; "The Ballad of Cesar Chavez," a modern *corrido* released in English and Spanish versions on the same 45; and a thunderous "Whittier Boulevard"–like instrumental, "Chicano Power." One of Willie G.'s first releases after his exit from the band was 1969's Latina-specific love song "Brown Baby."

As the first great wave of East L.A. bands began to move on, a younger generation of local musicians was coming up, drawing inspiration from the older musicians of the neighborhood.

"We had our local heroes in East L.A.," Cesar Rosas remembers. "Cannibal and the Headhunters and Thee Midniters and Ronnie and the Pomona Casuals and on and on and on. They made a big impression on us. They had records, they were recording already, so that's how we knew these guys. Of course, they played locally. In East L.A., it was a different scene. We would do dances. There were halls you could rent out, and these promoters would come in, like Huggy Boy and Eddie Torres, and put all these shows together. There weren't any venues where you could showcase your music. It was just kind of like a big party."

When Rosas and his high school friends finally joined the party as working musicians, it would be through the unlikely back door of folk music. But rock 'n' roll, straight out of the garage, was what they played first.

– 2 –

HOMEBOYS
Growing Up and Garfield

Though he came up playing the music of the day, Cesar Rosas had also been exposed to the traditional music of Mexico first, at its source. Unlike his future bandmates, he was an immigrant, from the Mexican state of Sonora, where his family had lived in considerable poverty.

"I grew up out in the desert—I didn't grow up in the city," Rosas remembers. "I remember every once in a while, there'd be a birthday or a special occasion. Of course, we didn't have running water, no electricity. They would bring a generator and bring in *norteño conjuntos*—accordion, *bajo sexto*, that kind of stuff. That was the very first time I ever heard live music, as a little boy."

The Rosas family immigrated to East Los Angeles in 1962, when Rosas was nine years old. As a boy, playing music was little more than a dream.

"I was kind of a late bloomer," he says. "I was more like a music lover first, and it wasn't until later that I started playing, actually playing guitar. As a young kid, I picked up the guitar and strummed it, but I couldn't play it. I always had the desire to play it, but I didn't know how to play it. I didn't know any chords or anything."

Before he became a musician, Rosas was a deeply involved fan: "I grew up listening to the Stones and the Beatles and Elvis Presley. Of course, [the '60s] was a pretty interesting time in the history of rock 'n' roll, because there was a lot of shit happening—Cream and Eric Clapton and Led Zeppelin and all that stuff. That was all there, too . . . Actually, I was a bigger fan of R&B stuff. KGFJ was the R&B station that I listened to. I was really a big fan of R&B stuff—James Brown to Aretha to Sam and Dave."

~~~~~~

In 1967, Rosas enrolled at East L.A.'s Robert Louis Stevenson Middle School, a block off Whittier Boulevard, where he met an already well-evolved musician, a guitarist named David Hidalgo.

"I met him in shop," says Rosas. "Dave was already playing guitar—he was an amazing guitar player already, as a kid. He could play all that Eric Clapton shit like nobody's business. He was great. We got to be friends in school. They had a talent show there, and of course Dave was there, he was performing. That's where I really realized he was a musician."

Hidalgo's parents were both first-generation Mexican Americans, born in Arizona; his fraternal grandfather was from Sonora, like Rosas. Born in Boyle Heights, he moved with his family to East L.A. in 1961. He began making music with his brother, who played drums and guitar.

"I started playing guitar when I was eleven," Hidalgo says. "At fourteen or fifteen, it actually started sounding like music to me. Before that, my fingers hurt, and I hated it. Then something opened the door and made me want to play guitar. I remember around that time, Hendrix, Canned Heat, Cream—that was the kind of stuff that got me excited about music.

"*Hit Parader* magazine used to have interviews with Clapton and guitar players I admired. They would always talk about people like [blues guitarists] Otis Rush and Elmore James that I hadn't heard. I started looking for it. I saw B. B. King on *The Steve Allen Show,* and that blew my mind. I had a friend of a friend at Garfield [High], and he was really into blues. I'd go over to his house and he'd play me all this stuff, and that's when I started getting into it."

Rosas and Hidalgo graduated from Stevenson in 1969 and moved to James A. Garfield High School in the heart of East L.A.

They had just missed a critical event in Chicano history that had played out there: in March 1968, Garfield was among the four East Side high schools where students walked out of classes to protest discriminatory inequities in education for Mexican American students.

Rosas says that he began getting serious about his guitar playing after he moved up to Garfield.

"There was this old parish that turned into what used to be called a teen post—there were a lot of those in L.A.," he recalls. "They catered to getting kids off the street and stuff like that. They had a little dancing class, and a few sports, and there was a little boxing thing. Then they had a guitar teacher. That's where I went. I had a guitar that belonged to my older brother Pete. It was an acoustic guitar. Actually, he started playing guitar before I did. So I decided that I would go ahead and pursue taking classes.

"I play the guitar the way that would be proper as a left-handed guitarist. In other words, [the guitar is strung] in the correct way—the mirror image of a right-handed player. My fingering was exactly the same fingering that a right-handed player would use, only left-handed. Jimi Hendrix strung his guitar properly, like I do . . . Albert King strung it upside down, and Otis Rush."

~~~~~~

At Garfield, Rosas and Hidalgo were joined by another Mexican American student, like them an aspiring musician, who transferred there in his sophomore year.

Louie Pérez's father was from Las Cruces, New Mexico; his mother was born near Mexico City. Pérez's parents had met on a cattle ranch in Cheyenne, Wyoming, where his maternal grandmother worked as a cook. In East L.A., the family predominantly spoke English at home; Pérez says, "They were immigrants, they came from Mexico, they knew what it was like, they knew how painful it was to try to assimilate. So they wanted us to speak English."

When Pérez was eight, his father died of a heart attack in the family's kitchen. From that point, music became an increasingly important part of his life.

"My mom was way into music," he remembers. "My mom loved *rancheras*, she loved Mexican music. It was usually coming out of the little Admiral radio on the kitchen sink counter, or she'd be playing records. She was always listening to records or listening to Mexican radio.

"My mom would take me on the bus down to the Million Dollar Theater on Broadway [in downtown Los Angeles]. They would have Mexican variety shows. My first experience with live music was sitting in the audience seeing this *mariachi* onstage. I swear there were about thirty-five of them. They would play, and the main attraction would come out—Miguel Aceves Mejia or Lola Beltrán or whoever, they'd come out onstage on horseback, the horse all covered with silver. It was shimmering in the stage lighting, and it was very surreal.

"I had this little plastic guitar that my grandmother gave me. My mom saw I was interested, so she saved her *centavos* and went down to Milan's Music Store on First Street and bought me my first guitar when I was probably ten or eleven. I think a couple of things were going on. She liked music. She wanted to encourage me to play music. The other thing was, it was her own youth diversion program. I lived in the *barrio* . . . It was kind of a tough neighborhood. My mom wanted to keep me away from hanging out on the street, so she figured, well, buy a guitar."

While Pérez took to the guitar, his mother's grander plan to keep her son from going astray went awry. After attending a Catholic elementary school, he was enrolled in Bishop Mora Salesian, the same school that many of Thee Midniters had attended.

"Halfway through the tenth grade," Pérez remembers, "I got called into the office because they did a routine sweep of the lockers and they found 165 joints in a rubber band in my locker. This is parochial school, private school. They said, 'We'll see you later, we're gonna call your mom, you're out of here.'"

After his expulsion, Pérez was forced to attend Garfield, his district's public high school. He quickly made friends with one of his art classmates, David Hidalgo.

Pérez says, "We sat in the back of the classroom, and they had these easel tables—it was basically like a school desk, and the tabletop lifted up. We'd lift up those easels so that we'd be completely blocked from the view of the teacher, and we would talk across the aisle, about records. 'Fairport Convention, you like them?' This was kind of weird music, because everybody was listening to Top 40. We were kind of the hippie guys. We were relating to all these cool records.

"I started going down to his pad to hang out, and the way I always tell it is, I moved into his house one day for about a year. [The Hidalgos] lived very close to the railroad tracks on Olympic, in this little house that was just kind of slapped together from parts of boxcars. It was a tiny little pad. We crammed into this one little room that was just big enough for him. It had a twin bed and a dresser and a black plastic Panasonic stereo, and we listened to records. Together we discovered Ry Cooder's *Into the Purple Valley*, and Steeleye Span, the Incredible String Band, a bunch of stuff. We started playing guitar together, and we started writing some songs. That's how it went."

On his own, Cesar Rosas had started to work with his own groups.

"There were a couple of friends around the corner that had already been playing for a little bit," he remembers. "I had a good buddy, and he was a bass player, and we got together and formed a little rock band. We were called the Young Sounds." He pauses in mid-recollection and laughs uproariously. "The *Young Sounds*, man! There we were. We had a bass player, a guitarist, myself, and a drummer. We started learning all the R&B stuff, and some rock stuff.

"I went ahead and formed another group called Fast Company, right around late '71. We played around L.A. and other places. It was a little bit more of a sophisticated R&B band, kind of like a Tower of Power R&B funk band. We used to play everything that was funk. It was a copy band—we didn't write too much of our own music, although I started writing a little bit back then.

It was a dance club band. We played around the East Side a lot, like the Kennedy Hall, the Big Union [Hall in Vernon], the Little Union. There were a couple of clubs in downtown L.A. They were dance clubs. There was La Pantera Rosa, the Red Onion, the Quiet Cannon, the Mardi Gras. They were over-21 clubs—we had fake IDs and stuff."

~~~~~~

At the same time that Cesar was cutting his soulful groove with Fast Company, another, slightly older musician from Garfield was making a rep for himself on the club and concert scene.

Conrad Lozano lived on the boundary between the Belvedere and City Terrace neighborhoods in East L.A. His parents were American-born—his mother from El Paso, his father from Cypress, California. "My folks spoke Spanish, but they never spoke it very often around me," Lozano says.

Some members of Lozano's family liked music—his half brother was an Elvis Presley fan, his Anglo cousin loved Johnny Cash, another cousin played surf music, and his uncle played Hawaiian-style steel guitar. But Mexican music was not a part of the diet, and little music was played at home.

He took up the bass as a student at Belvedere Junior High. "My mom would listen to things like Herb Alpert and the Tijuana Brass, which was probably kind of good for me," he says. "That was the first music I learned how to play on the electric bass, because it was the only music I had available to me, where I could put on a record and repeat the music and learn how to play the bass better."

Recruited by a classmate, Lozano joined his first high school band, Connie and the Royal Men, whose lineup included a female drummer and the keyboardist Eric Johns, later of the disco group Heatwave. A succession of other groups followed: the Young Beats, the Extremes (a British Invasion cover band), the Royal Checkmates (a soul unit). In 1968–1969, he played in his best-known East L.A. combo, Euphoria, a heavy power trio that covered Cream, Blue Cheer, and the Jimi Hendrix Experience.

"We were playing almost every weekend," Lozano says. "We played for car clubs, private parties. We played different functions. We even played for a few weddings. We played dances. We played Kennedy Hall. We played the East L.A. Battles of the Bands. We did all kinds of stuff. That band actually lasted about two years. We were very busy."

Euphoria played loud enough that the band's rehearsals could be heard throughout the neighborhood, according to Pérez. "I was a closet musician for a while," he says. "Conrad was my neighbor, and I'd walk up the hill—it was like three blocks—and watch the band rehearse at his house."

After Euphoria disbanded, Lozano cast around for other work, and played sporadically with a run of East L.A. outfits. Finally, in 1971—a year after his belated mid-term graduation from Garfield—he was recruited by drummer Kenny Román, with whom he'd played in a Whittier-based act called Bosco, to audition for a new group fronted by Stevie and Rudy Salas. The brothers were East Side music *veteranos* who had recorded for Eddie Davis and been members of El Chicano, the unit that had scored a Top 30 national hit with their 1970 version of big band leader Gerald Wilson's instrumental "Viva Tirado."

"For about two years I was with Tierra," says Lozano, who appeared on the group's 1973 debut album. "We were recording, we were touring, and that was my main thing."

The others had followed Lozano out of Garfield—Pérez graduated in 1971, while Hidalgo and Rosas received their diplomas in 1972. Rosas continued to busy himself with Fast Company. Hidalgo and Pérez enrolled in Los Angeles City College and then East L.A. College, as they dabbled together in garage band projects like the Checkers and the Variety.

Then, one by one, these young rock 'n' rollers were enlisted in a very different sort of musical project.

- 3 -

A BEGINNING

The Founding of Los Lobos
del Este de Los Angeles

One bright summer afternoon in 1973, fate strolled by Cesar Rosas's front door.

"I was hanging out in my garage, and all of a sudden midday one day I saw this guy walking right in front of my house on the sidewalk. He was walking around playing the mandolin. He was going to the store. He was passing by. He looked inside the garage. We looked and kind of waved . . . I said, 'What are you up to?' He said, 'Well, I'm going to Pomona College.' I said, 'I see you play mandolin and all that.' He was getting into Mexican music, playing traditional music."

The rotund, mandolin-strumming twenty-year-old with a drooping *bandito* mustache was named Frank González, and he lived two doors down the street from Rosas.

Like the rest of his soon-to-be bandmates, González was raised in East L.A. His father had emigrated from Mexico at the age of four, returned to his home country at the age of fifteen, and came back to Los Angeles with a young bride.

The last of seven children and known as Frank from boyhood, he grew up in a musical household. "My father had been a professional singer, a trained singer," González recalls. "I have posters of him doing some *zarzuela* [Spanish opera] at theaters in downtown L.A. during the '40s. He was a tenor." His brothers both played guitar, and his four sisters sang. He began playing autoharp and harmonica in the first grade, and started formal training on trombone in third grade. After developing an allergy to the metal in his mouthpiece, he took up the upright bass, which he played throughout junior high. At Garfield High School, he met another budding bassist, Conrad Lozano.

González formed his first band, Boojum Snark—its name drawn from a backwoods spirit mentioned in a blood-brother oath on *The Andy Griffith Show*—with another Garfield student, his longtime friend David Hidalgo. The guitarist notes that even as a youth, years before Rosas saw him playing on the street, González favored performing alfresco.

"We had met in elementary school," Hidalgo recalls. "He lived about five or six blocks away from where I lived. Around fifth or sixth grade, [I saw him] walking down the street with his guitar or something . . . I went over to his pad one day, and he was sitting in his Boy Scout uniform, playing Bob Dylan songs."

Like Hidalgo's other early bands, Boojum Snark never emerged from the garage. González graduated from Garfield in 1971 and enrolled in Pomona College in Claremont, then something of a hotbed for the Chicano arts, to study music and musicology. Always eclectic in his tastes, he played country music (he had become facile on the Dobro), performed classical works, and worked as a bassist with such avant-garde jazz lions as saxophonist David Murray. But, he says, "everything that I was doing, it was always everybody else's [music]."

His musical revelation arrived via his classmate and roommate Gustavo Gil, a Colombia-born pianist whose father had an extensive collection of Colombian and Mexican folk music. He became entranced by a folk dance style popular in the country's northern provinces.

"The first time I started getting into a *huapango* and actually playing it," González says, "it was like in *The Wizard of Oz*, when it goes from black-and-white to color. I wasn't in Kansas anymore. I was in a whole different world, and it just blew me away. Especially when I realized that I could sing it and I could play it."

González's enthusiasm for Mexican folk styles burgeoned rapidly. He began acquiring information on the music's instrumentation from Charles Chase at the Claremont Folk Music

Center. In 1972, Gonzalez and Gil journeyed to Mexico City and Veracruz. "That was the first time I saw *jarocho* music [the regional style of Veracruz] played live. It really blew me away," he says. "It was like Mexican bebop, and I loved bebop."

In mid-1973, González says without elaboration, "it was a very, very dark time for me," so he took a medical leave from Pomona College. It was at just that point that he encountered Cesar Rosas. The two young musicians quickly discovered they both had an affinity for Mexican folk music, and González was surprised by the somewhat younger musician's knowledge of the repertoire.

"I invited him over to the house, and we got to know each other," Rosas says. "He was playing the mandolin, and he played me a riff from a song. He said, 'Do you know this song?' I said, 'Yeah, I know that song.' I was a rural Mexican guy—I knew all about all the folk songs. I said, 'Yeah, I grew up with that. I know what that song is.' I sang it to him a little bit. He was slightly impressed. I said, 'That's what I listen to every morning when I get up to go to school, on the radio.' So we were talking the same language.

"It didn't take too long for us to start talking about music and sharing music. He was on vacation and I was on vacation. The next day he invited me over for a beer, and I took over my Spanish guitar. We started jamming together on traditional songs. We were just learning the songs. Of course I grew up with them, but I really didn't know how to play them. Playing that type of music requires a certain type of strum. It's the *huapango* rhythm—it's the way you strum the guitar for a lot of those old songs. He kind of knew how to play the rhythm, and he showed me how to play it. Before you know it, he and I were playing two or three songs together. There we were, singing and harmonizing and playing guitar, and he was playing the mandolin parts. We'd make it to the middle of the song, and then it'd fall apart. Then we'd start it again."

Rosas and González began getting together regularly in an attempt to teach themselves the fundamentals of the Mexican folk styles. There was a great seriousness of intent on González's part.

"I was very active in the Chicano movement," he says. "One of the things that struck me as kinda weird was, everybody was [saying] 'Chicano power,' but then they'd go listen to Santana or Tito Puente, and that was being Chicano. We were surrounded by Mexican music, but we didn't want to identify with that. That was [for] the *wetbacks*, that was not us, right? . . . There was only two ways we were allowed to identify. You could play white rock 'n' roll, or oldies, stuff like that, East L.A.–type music, or if you wanted to be [singing in] Spanish, you had to be dressed up in your monkey suit and be a *mariachi*. The young kids were being told what to do by a coterie of mainly white guys, telling them how to play Mexican music. *Mariachi* music was acceptable, because that was middle class. But the *norteño* stuff, that wasn't cool. The *tejano* stuff, that was not cool."

In time, the two musicians were joined at Rosas's parents' home by Fast Company's bassist, Robert Becerra, for informal living room sessions. At the time González was concentrating on his mandolin chops; Cesar thought it might be interesting to enlist another string player, and suggested their mutual friend David Hidalgo.

Rosas says, "I told Frank, 'Hey, why don't I call Dave?' So I called Dave one afternoon and he came over. We started shooting the breeze, and Dave had never seen that [music]. He looked at us and said, 'Wow, that's kinda cool.' Up until then, Dave was playing just steel-string guitar . . . I don't recall him playing any kind of folk instrument."

While Hidalgo was well aware of the cultural context in which González was formulating his ideas, he came to Mexican music—a style almost wholly unknown to him—through the backdoor of the American and Anglo-American folk–rock of the late '60s.

"At that time, it was the Chicano Renaissance," Hidalgo remembers. "The muralists and more literature started developing. Frank kind of came up with the idea, the whole cultural awareness thing. Being a musician, it seemed like a natural place to go. For me, at that time the Band was happening, and

Fairport Convention. There was that folk–rock stuff. Especially Fairport—I really liked the *Full House* band, where they were doing jigs and reels with electric guitars. That's what got me started thinking about folk music more than electric guitar stuff.

"I started out with mandolin. I wanted to play mandolin, so this would give me an excuse to learn. We all started at the bottom. We listened to records and learned a few songs. The more we got into it, we discovered that there was more to it."

González says, "I showed Dave some stuff, and he said, 'Yeah. How about [bringing in] Louie?' So I said, 'Well, OK, bring Louie.' So we started learning some tunes."

After Louie Pérez joined the living room ensemble as a guitarist, he also became intoxicated by a music that was at once a bedrock part of his Mexican American culture and far outside the hometown mainstream. Even though he was aware of some of the music from his boyhood, he experienced a revelation when he started to listen seriously to it and perform it.

Pérez says, "Here were these kids who were discovering Mexican music, and it was, 'Wow, where did all this come from?' As the soundtrack to our lives, it played as the underscore . . . When we listened to Trio Los Panchos and listened to the *requinto* player, we said, 'Shit, this guy is blowing away Jimmy Page!' We had discovered this thing that was literally in our backyards—it was over there by that tree, but we had never paid attention to it. This whole thing opened up. We were literally like kids in candy stores, learning how to play these instruments, finding them. We didn't know how to tune them, we didn't know what they were. 'Wow, there's one!' We picked up this stuff for like fifteen bucks as everybody else was buying Stratocasters."

Richard "Fish" Escalante, a friend of Pérez's, was soon brought in to replace bassist Becerra, whose style was not to González's liking. Escalante had a notable pedigree: his father, Nick Escalante, was the bassist in Desi Arnaz's jazzy Latin orchestra, and had appeared on Arnaz and Lucille Ball's hugely popular '50s sitcom *I Love Lucy* as a member of Ricky Ricardo's band.

Over time, the young musicians added more and more

instruments to their arsenal, schooling themselves as they went. Pérez began to play *jarana* (a small-bodied, percussive eight-stringed guitar), *quinto* (a ten-stringed guitar), and *vihuela* (a twelve-stringed Spanish instrument, also played occasionally by Cesar); Hidalgo picked up the violin, mandola (a large-bodied mandolin), *bajo sexto* (the large-bodied twelve-string, a sideline for Cesar as well), and *requinto jarocho* (a distinctive four-stringed box plucked with a plectrum); and González dedicated himself to mastering the Veracruz harp.

In the hunt for the music, Hidalgo remembers, "we'd go all over L.A. to all the little markets. You'd go to a market or a drugstore, and they had a record rack, all over East L.A. It was two bucks a record. You could create this whole collection of cool stuff."

Adds Rosas, "We bought a lot of the traditional records at the liquor store. We were doing this for fun. We didn't know what the hell we were doing. We didn't really call it a band yet. We were just popping beers, man, and having a good time. It was like a celebration of this folk music. It was like a bluegrass group. It was a joyous thing and a cool thing, because we were playing authentic Mexican music."

Some older and more experienced local musicians had a hand in the fledgling, self-taught group's education. Hidalgo says, "After we started playing around town, playing *tamaladas* [tamale-making parties], afternoon shows, or playing colleges, we'd see these musicians who were around, and they saw us. They'd say, 'Ah, I like what you're trying to do. But you're not doing it right.' These guys started taking us under their wings, and they actually started to show us the instruments, the different rhythmic patterns, stuff like that, to get it going."

He specifically acknowledges Art Gerst as an important early influence. Gerst, a graduate of UCLA's ethnomusicology department, was for years the harpist and violinist in Los Camperos, a local mariachi unit that held a regular, extremely popular gig at La Fonda, a Mexican restaurant abutting MacArthur Park in L.A.'s largely Hispanic Westlake district. "He was the one who said, 'I like what you're trying to do, let me help you,'" Hidalgo says. "He was the one who got me started on violin."

Sometime in late 1973—the exact date is lost to history—the group made their first public appearance, courtesy of Fernando "Fernie" Mosqueda, a friend of one of Frank González's brothers who was deeply involved in East L.A. community organizations.

Rosas recalls with amusement, "One day Fernie came over and knocked at the door. We were playing in Frank's living room and couldn't hear him knocking. We stopped and said, 'Hey, there's someone at the door, right?' So Fernie walked in, and said, 'Hey, that was a cool song. Where can I get that record?' He thought that we had the record player on . . . We all started laughing and said, 'That was *us*.' And he said, 'Get the fuck outta here! No!' He thought we were joking. So we ended up playing him a song, and his jaw hit the floor. He goes, 'What the fuck! This is amazing!'

"He was going to be involved in coordinating an event for this senior citizens group to be held in the next couple of weeks. It was a fund-raiser for them. It was to be held over in Watts. So he kept begging us—he said, 'Hey, you guys gotta play this thing. I've got this thing coming up. It's just a benefit for little old ladies. They're gonna make tamales.' We said, 'Get the fuck outta here, Fernie. We know like seven songs, and we're not even a band. We're just here having a few beers.' But he convinced us. And we were in terror."

Now that they had a gig, the untested, unnamed Mexican folk ensemble also needed a professional moniker. González says, "At one of the rehearsals at Cesar's house, we were joking about the name. [Someone] said [it should be] Wolfie and the Wombats, because Dave's nickname was Wolfie. [In those days, the bearded, long-haired Hidalgo bore a striking resemblance to the Wolf Man, as incarnated by Lon Chaney, Jr.] And [we had] an album by Los Lobos del Norte, which was a pretty well-known group."

As Rosas recalls it, "I said, 'Hey, how about Los Lobos?' Because all of these Mexican groups like Los Tigres del Norte . . . named themselves after wildlife and shit, or birds and shit. I said, 'Why don't we call it Los Lobos?'"

In González's recollection, "I said, 'No, no, we're Los Lobos del Este de Los Angeles. We're the Lobos of East L.A. That's where we came from.'"

On a Saturday at noon, Rosas, Hidalgo, Pérez, Escalante, and González—the newly christened Wolves of East L.A.—rolled up to the *tamalada* at the Veterans of Foreign Wars Hall in Watts in the van Cesar usually used to haul Fast Company's gear.

Rosas remembers fondly, "It was the old days, the cool days, when you could drive into Watts and everything was copacetic, especially with Chicanos. We walked up there, the doors were open and you could see the little old ladies walking around carrying trays and getting stuff together for this afternoon event that we were supposed to play at. So I walk in, and the lady says, 'Can I help you, *amigo*? Are you delivering?' I said, 'No, we're the musicians.' We're little hippies, we have our beards and long hair, right? And we're dressed in just normal clothes. Another little old lady comes by and says, 'Oh, it's the musicians! They're here to set up.' As we walk in, I hear one lady ask the other, 'Well, where are their *mariachi* suits?' 'Oh, I don't know, Sarah. They'll probably put 'em on later after they're set up.'

"So here comes showtime. Here we are, dressed in regular clothes and little beards and long hair. I had my little PA from my rock band Fast Company, and we set it up. We hit the first chord. *Bam!* And you should have seen their faces, man. They were so thrilled. All those little old-timers and shit, they started dancing immediately. It was an instant party. There we were. We had seven, eight, nine songs, and we did 'em like three times. We kept repeating them. We were on our way. We'd signed our first little contract. We had a name. We were a band."

"There was a whole bunch of Vietnam vets there," González remembers. "We went into the bar area. These veterans saw us, and they were ready to kill us [because of] the way we looked. This was '73, '74. We all had longer hair. They all saw us as evil hippie types. But when we started playing, when we did *boleros* and stuff, they dug it. They accepted it. They said, 'OK, this is cool.'"

The *tamalada* appearance was successful enough that Mosqueda decided to book Los Lobos del Este de Los Angeles into other, similar venues, and became the group's first, ad hoc manager.

By universal testimony, "Fish" Escalante was a hard-partying individual who couldn't be counted on to make rehearsals or gigs regularly. So Los Lobos turned to another musician to fill in: Escalante's best friend and Pérez's old neighborhood pal, Conrad Lozano, a frequent visitor at the group's rehearsals, and fortunately a quick study.

"Fish wouldn't show up at rehearsals—he was too loaded," González says. "Finally, one time, we had a gig. This was around the third or fourth gig. Fish didn't come, and Conrad said, 'I can do it.' So he jumped in and started playing."

Lozano says, "They got a little gig, after maybe a month of practicing or playing together. They needed to get a rehearsal done on Friday or Thursday so that they could do this little gig on Saturday. And Richard didn't show up. It just so happened that I was home and I wasn't working that weekend. They said, 'Hey, man, we need somebody to sit in with us,' and I said, 'Just tell me what I gotta do.'"

In early 1974, while maintaining his lucrative role in Tierra, Lozano permanently replaced his unreliable buddy in the neophyte folk act. Los Lobos del Este de Los Angeles soon found themselves with plenty of work on the East Side.

"We did a lot of schools," Hidalgo says. "Fernie thought, 'Wow, man, this would work doing it at school assemblies, Cinco de Mayo,' that sort of thing. That was how we got into all the schools. He had friends all over East L.A. We worked at the different high schools and junior highs."

Says González, "It turned people's heads around. They didn't know what to think, because we were doing something they never thought they'd see. At the city schools, the teachers would just be blown away."

Pérez says one function was a financial mainstay for the band: "If you are a Chicano and you got married between 1973 and 1980, we probably played your wedding. We never had a Saturday off in all of that time, because we were always playing weddings."

"We would even play funerals—people wanted us to play the traditional stuff at funerals," Lozano says. He adds with a laugh, "We even played for a bar mitzvah one time! It was cool. This guy loved the band so much. He wanted something different at his son's bar mitzvah, and he had us play.

"For about five or six years, we got involved with the universities," Lozano adds. "At that time, you've got to realize, the Chicano awareness was coming about. People were really wanting to get into their roots, Mexican roots. The colleges were really, really promoting that. They heard about Los Lobos. And when we first started, there were only a few bands that were actually doing that. We were doing it. There was another band from San Diego called Los Allegranes who were also doing that—they decided they wanted to learn their roots and play the Mexican folk stuff. But they were more hardcore than we were, because we were more rock 'n' roll–based, right, whereas these guys were closer to the border, so they were more *Mexicano*-based."

In the first couple of years of their existence—as the burgeoning *Chicanismo* movement led to the growth of organizations like Movimiento Estudiantil Chicano de Aztlán (MEChA), the Latino student group—Los Lobos del Este de Los Angeles began to reap large seasonal dividends from their work.

"Every May, around Cinco de Mayo, we'd load up the van and go all over the place and play for 150 bucks here, 300 bucks there," Pérez says. "We called this 'the Dash for Cash.' During that period, there were so many things going on, and we were kind of the go-to band for that kind of stuff. We would go for a couple of weeks, playing up and down California for all these MEChA groups and Chicano community organizations that were having celebrations around Cinco de Mayo."

Around this time, the band members became so fixated with the music that they explored it at its source. Rosas says, "It got to the point where we all got on the bus and went to Mexico, collected instruments, studied with old-timers. We got very involved on the folk side of things. We learned where it came

from, we learned everything about it. We were *folkloristas* . . .
We were absorbing everything. We became like students, and
just went to school with it."

By 1975, the band had attained enough prominence in East L.A.'s
Mexican American community that they became the subject
of a half-hour episode of *La Cultura*, a weekly series aimed at
Latinos that was telecast by the Los Angeles PBS outlet, KCET.
The show, which can be viewed in its entirety on YouTube, is the
earliest look at Los Lobos as a working band, and the only known
documentation of González's time with the group.

After a brief montage shot on East L.A.'s streets, Los Lobos
del Este de Los Angeles are seen rehearsing on a hillside below
Conrad Lozano's house. Downtown L.A. is visible in the distance. Sporting shoulder-length hair, bearded and mustachioed,
the band members smoke cigarettes and drink beer; their friend
Ernesto Reyes sits with the group, bumming a cigarette off Rosas
and cradling in his lap a rooster that lived in the Lozanos' yard.
Lozano is seen playing the *guitarron*, the large-bodied Mexican
bass guitar played over-the-shoulder style, which he had by then
added to his instrumental arsenal. In a voice-over, González
explains, "We got together to learn some songs to play for our
mothers, to show them we appreciated the music of our culture
. . . Now we feel it's an obligation to spread our culture to the
other people who don't know about it." He continues, "We want
to make a true Chicano music that draws from our past, that is
in line with the past, the present, and hopefully the future."

At this juncture, Los Lobos were clearly still very much
González's band. In the sequence showing the band in rehearsal,
it is he who guides the other members through the material,
fine-tuning the technical elements of the performances. The
majority of the show is drawn from a concert date, probably
typical of the Lobos' early institutional appearances, filmed
at East Los Angeles College. González takes all but one of the
lead vocals and serves as the emcee for the set, introducing the
songs (some of which would appear on the group's debut album

two years later) and, at the program's end, introducing (with a note of mockery) the other band members—Rosas as "the 'Sabor a Mi' Kid" (for his primary role as the group's *bolero* soloist), Hidalgo as "El Tomate" (for his rosy complexion). Pérez briefly takes the microphone to introduce González as "the founding member of the group."

As the closing credits roll, González says to the concert audience, "We're Los Lobos del Este de Los Angeles—just another band from East L.A." That self-effacing appellation—a nod to the Mothers of Invention's 1972 album *Just Another Band from L.A.*, and to the Mothers' leader, Frank Zappa, co-author of "Memories of El Monte," the Penguins' 1963 homage to East L.A. R&B shows—would become the title of Los Lobos' debut album. But by that time, Frank González was no longer a member of the group he had co-founded.

He admits that his escalating alcoholism had made him the odd man out in his own band.

"I was drinking a lot," he says. "Alcohol has a lot to do with a lot of things that happened in that band . . . I was very unhappy. At one point I got really sick and I couldn't play. Finally I got so sick that I'd literally fall off the stage."

Rosas, who was the only member of the band with a driver's license at that point, had to pick up González for the band's gigs, and witnessed his deterioration intimately: "I'm knocking at the door, and he's wiped out. I had to get him up and shower him up, like in the movies . . . I was always taking care of Frank, and Frank was falling apart. He had a lot of demons, he had a lot of problems. And of course it started to manifest itself in the band."

The tension between González and his bandmates finally detonated during a showdown in late 1976 at "the clubhouse," a small house—built by Pérez's father behind the family home and formerly occupied by the musician's grandmother—that the group used for rehearsals.

Pérez says, "We had this big blowout. It just blew up at rehearsal one day, and everybody was really bummed out. Frank was certainly really bummed out. It was over something that was really stupid that didn't even have anything to do with [the band]. It was over some pot or something that somebody had bought, somebody who was a friend of ours who was hanging out with a friend of his. It really wasn't initiated by something that happened between us. But it became a personal thing, and he walked out, and just quit, and that was it.

"He was our musical director, he was our lead singer, he was our front man guy, and to a certain degree he was a bit of a dictator. When he left, there was a little bit of 'Ding-Dong! The Witch Is Dead' kind of shit. I really think he thought the band could not survive, but we said, 'Hey, well, we're just going to do this.' And we just kept doing it."

After his abrupt exit from Los Lobos, Frank González slowly set about remaking his personal and professional life. He ultimately embraced sobriety in 1981, and married in 1984. For a time, he served as musical director for El Teatro Campesino, the highly politicized Latino theater group founded by writer–director Luis Valdez, who would himself play an important role in Los Lobos' career. González later established himself as a solo performer of regional Mexican and Chicano music and marketed a line of custom-made instrument strings. Today a Tucson resident, he has worked as an arranger for Ronstadt Generations, the group led by Linda Ronstadt's younger brother Michael. For more than a decade, he has been collaborating on a projected autobiography of Mexican *jarocho* harpist Mario Barradas Murcia. He has returned to his own cultural roots.

"I stopped going by Frank and went back to using my real name, which is Francisco," he says. "I didn't even know my real name until I was older. Nobody ever called me Francisco. For me it was like, OK, I've changed. That [other] guy died. That person really did die."

In 2009, Francisco González released *The Gift/El Regalo*, a beautiful album of solo performances on the Veracruz harp, co-produced by the well-known bassist Harvey Brooks. Among its thirteen tracks was "De Colores," a traditional number that also appeared as the first track of the 1976 album on which Los Lobos made their first recorded appearance. It was also the only number González ever recorded with the band he founded.

– 4 –

RECORDING *POR LA RAZA*

The Making of *Si Se Puede!*
and *Just Another Band from East L.A.*

Art Brambila, the entrepreneur who brought Los Lobos del Este de Los Angeles into the studio for the first time, was a hustler. Some in Los Lobos' camp might use even less flattering terms. But there can be no doubt that Brambila attacked his goals with a combination of drive, ambition, and chutzpah. To an extent he was to the early '70s what Eddie Davis, the Anglo entrepreneur whose Rampart Records recorded a host of top East L.A. bands, was to the '60s.

Many of the pertinent details of Brambila's career are laid out by Mark Guerrero, the musician son of Lalo Guerrero, in a well-researched piece based on a 2011 interview that appears on his website. Born and raised in Lincoln Heights on the East Side, Brambila grew up a gangbanger, but an interest in music was his salvation. His nephews, and neighbors, were Steve and Rudy Salas.

Breaking into the record business in Capitol Records' marketing department, Brambila began scouting talent for the label. He moved into management, handling Mark Guerrero, Yaqui, Carmen Moreno, and, most important, Tierra, the band founded by the Salas brothers after their stint with El Chicano. He also promoted concerts in East L.A.

The mid-'70s found Brambila working for ABC-TV and later as director of Motown Latino, a short-lived imprint for such acts as José Feliciano. In 1976, inspired while watching *Soul Train*, he envisioned an unprecedented enterprise that would combine his expertise in TV and music: a youth-oriented Latino dance show. Using his considerable ingenuity, he secured money and facilities from the Spanish-language L.A. station KMEX to shoot a pilot. Tierra was booked for the episode, and Brambila convinced Tex–Mex star Freddy Fender and salsa luminary Tito Puente to appear.

But Brambila needed a sponsor to sell his package. Knowing that Cesar Chavez, the president of the United Farm Workers, enjoyed a relationship with Coca-Cola, the nervy promoter called Chavez, whom he had never met or spoken to, and set up a meeting with the legendary Chicano union activist in Northern California. After a screening of the pilot, Chavez agreed to call the soft drink company on Brambila's behalf. Coke expressed an interest in sponsoring the program, and with an agreement in hand Brambila secured a thirteen-week run for his show, *The Mean Salsa Machine*, with L.A.'s local TV outlet KHJ.

According to Mark Guerrero, in 1976 Brambila came up with the idea of creating a benefit album to support the UFW's organizing and community efforts. It would be called *Sí Se Puede!* after the union's longtime motto, "Yes We Can!"

It was only natural that Los Lobos del Este de Los Angeles would be recruited as the project's house band, which would back a variety of singers, from Brambila's clients Carmen Moreno and the Salas brothers to a group of fourth- and fifth-grade students from East L.A.'s School of Santa Isabel. The group exhibited the kind of versatility necessary to support performers working in a plethora of styles. Also, most of the material for the album was based in traditional folk; with three years of playing Mexican folk music under their belts, there was no other band in East L.A. that could compete with the Lobos' virtuosity.

Los Lobos del Este de Los Angeles were undoubtedly familiar to the UFW's principals, thanks to their runs up and down the California coast during Cinco de Mayo season. They were also well known to Daniel Valdez, brother of Luis Valdez, who was Cesar Chavez's right-hand man during the UFW's early days of organizing in the '60s.

"In 1974, Los Lobos did a major show with Daniel Valdez,"

Lozano says. "Daniel had a record out on A&M [*Mestizo*, released in 1973], and he was promoting it and he was doing a show at the San Gabriel Civic Auditorium. They had heard about what we were doing, and they invited us to come down and play."

Lozano says that Art Brambila was apparently in the house that night, and his presence led to the bassist's precipitous exit from Tierra for full-time work with Los Lobos.

"He reported back to the band, 'Hey, your bass player is moonlighting out there.' I went to rehearsal [on the following] Tuesday and set up my amp and everything. Then we start talking: 'Hey, man, we hear that you're playing with this other band called Los Lobos. What are you doing? It's either gonna be that band or this band.' They gave me the ultimatum. I said, 'You know what? *Fuck* you guys.' I packed up my bass and left. They were in the middle of making a record, too. And I'm not sorry that I did it."

By the time Brambila was putting together *Si Se Puede!* any bad blood engendered by Lozano's angry departure had apparently dissipated. At that point, the other members of Los Lobos had also started to devote themselves full-time to their acoustic work: Pérez and Hidalgo had abandoned Catchow, a garage Top 40 group with Jesse Velo (later the bassist for the East L.A. punk band Los Illegals), and Rosas had disbanded Fast Company.

Los Lobos managed to record a single track with Frank González, "De Colores," before the wrangle at rehearsal led to his departure. The group is collectively credited with the arrangements, in which González certainly had a hand. The rest of the tracks on which the group participated marked the first appearance of the four-piece lineup of Rosas, Hidalgo, Pérez, and Lozano.

The album was cut at A&M, the top-flight Hollywood facility on the like-named label's lot (which formerly housed Charlie Chaplin's movie studio) at Sunset Boulevard and La Brea Avenue, on time contributed by the label's co-founder Herb Alpert. As a result, it's a crisp, professional-sounding recording, cleanly produced by Brambila.

Today the recording survives as something of a period piece, though it is no more or less dated than, say, the pro-labor songs cut by Woody Guthrie and Pete Seeger's Almanac Singers in the '40s. There are musical homages to Chavez and UFW co-founder Dolores Huerta; a version of the old labor union rabble-rouser "We Shall Not Be Moved" (sung in Spanish and titled "No Nos Moveran"); and sentimental pro-labor narration (by Alfonso Tafoya of the Latino group Nosotros) layered atop the traditional "De Colores," which is sung by the children's choir.

For their lone solo moment, Los Lobos blast through the album's shortest track, a revision of the traditional *son jarocho* "Tilingo Lingo." Clocking in at 1:52, it's a lively double-time rendition, sung in Spanish, of the Veracruz dance tune with lead vocals by Rosas, who contributes a series of *gritos* (cries) and squeals. Uncredited new lyrics were penned for the occasion:

> *Meanwhile we are on strike*
> *We cannot eat grapes*
> *How can we eat salads*
> *Because of the lettuce strike*

The song's original lyrics contain a prophetic reference to another, better-known *son jarocho*: "To dance *tilingo lingo* . . . one dances in the manner of *la bamba*."

Though the members of Los Lobos were no doubt pleased to be associated with the union that had become the most prominent expression of Chicano political power to date, Hidalgo says that despite founding member Frank González's ties to the Chicano movement, Los Lobos del Este de Los Angeles remained resolutely opposed to presenting themselves as a political unit, but instead viewed their work as cultural in nature.

"The fact that we were young Chicanos from the East Side playing this music was enough of a statement," Hidalgo says. "That was our involvement. We'd play these things with all these political bands, and they would be like, 'Preach to the people.' [We'd say,] 'We don't have to. We don't want to. The music is enough.'"

Adds Pérez, "We weren't politicized at all. [The movement] was going on at the same time. Once we formed Los Lobos and started playing, locals and people who were more politicized picked up on us, and they were pushing for us to become more politicized. Even though we played for Cesar Chavez and played a lot of stuff for MEChA . . . we stuck to the music part. There were a lot of groups who modeled themselves after us, who were activists first and musicians second. We were musicians first."

~~~~~~

A hint about where Los Lobos del Este de Los Angeles were headed can be found in the group's bio in the notes to *Si Se Puede!* "They have appeared on many television programs, and have done background music on many films including *Una Familia.*"

Like a good deal of the information in those liner notes, this isn't quite correct. The group's TV appearances had at that point been limited to *La Cultura* and one or two other local public TV shots. The film was in fact titled *The Pedrosa Family,* and it had been directed by the man who would become the producer of the band's first album.

Long before he became a well-known broadcaster at KNX in Los Angeles, Luis Torres was an aspiring industrial filmmaker. He recalls that in 1974 or '75, when he was a journalism school student, his friend Adolfo "Rudy" Vargas, a graduate of Garfield High, was working on a degree at UCLA's School of Film and Television.

Torres recalls, "He needed music for this little industrial film, and he said, 'Man, I've heard that these guys—these kind of hippie Chicano guys—they're playing *Mexicano* music. They're playing mandolins and guitars, but they're real good!' I said, 'Who are they?' He said, 'I don't know. I think they call themselves Los Lobos, I'm not sure.' He had a phone number for one of the guys, a guy named Louie Pérez. So I called Louie and told him, 'We need some music. Would you guys want to do some music for this little industrial film?'"

Vargas and Torres employed the group, which still numbered Frank González among its members, to create the music for a couple of shorts in 1975–1976.

"I did a little film for the University of California," Torres says. "It was a recruitment film—a film to encourage Chicanos to apply to college. I got a little bit of money that was funneled through the Chicano Studies Center. It was an organized research unit at University of California, Santa Barbara. We recorded in Santa Barbara in one of the university studios. It was one of the first times I'd ever really recorded anything. They recorded incidental music for this little film.

"Then we also did a little film called *The Pedrosa Family*, a little ethnographic film . . . It was a film paid for by an organization, or a business really, called Bilingual Educational Services. They were making filmstrips and movies and books for the bilingual education market. It was a cinema verité thing about a family in Arizona, in Tucson I think. It follows this little kid. It's a documentary, sort of a coming-of-age thing."

It was during the making of the latter film that Torres, who had limited exposure to Los Lobos' live performances at that point, realized the depth of the group's abilities: "The movie ended with the father of this little kid and his *compadre* sitting in a garage drinking beer and playing, very poorly, an old *corrido*, 'Rayito de Luna.' We had a flatbed editing table, and Dave Hidalgo was [watching the scene]. The idea was, let's let these two guys in the garage play the music, and then let Dave start playing the song, fade down the bad playing of the old guys and let Dave do these licks, and then we run the credits over it.

"Dave just sat there—he'd never heard the song—and then immediately he figured out the chords. As the Moviola was going, here's Dave playing these amazing licks, playing off that melody, doing something that Clapton would have been proud of. I'm not a musician, and I thought, 'Man! That's just amazing!' I had a guitar and I played a little bit, very, very poorly. It would take me a day to half-assed learn a song. Dave Hidalgo in one minute had this thing down. I thought, 'Jeez, these guys know how to play.'"

The association with Los Lobos continued after Torres and Vargas formed a small production company, New Vista, with another young Latino filmmaker, Jesus Treviño (later a prolific director for such TV series as *NYPD Blue*, *Star Trek: Voyager*, and *Babylon 5*), and a Cal State, L.A. administrator with film aspirations named David Sandoval.

"The four of us made a few films, mostly industrial films. We did some things for public television. It was a little company, sort of seat-of-our-pants stuff. We went from little project to little project. Jesus Treviño and I got a grant from the Los Angeles County Department of Health Services, the health department, to make some films on alcoholism. We used Los Lobos for one of those films. That was about '77.

"We barely survived. But we got some money together and we bankrolled this idea—let's do an album with these guys, to create a calling card for them, basically. It would help them get gigs, and help them, we hoped, get the attention of maybe a record company, and a record deal."

According to Lozano, the New Vista partners' inspiration came at the right time: "We didn't have the money to put a record together. We really wanted to do it, but we didn't have the means to do it. Luis Torres and David Sandoval became a little close to Louie at that time. They'd come around a lot. We started talking about it, so they thought, 'Well, maybe we can figure out a way to help them out.' So they were able to come up with the means to record it in a studio."

The humble nature of the project, which was largely financed out of David Sandoval's pocket, can be dramatically seen in a budget reproduced in the 2000 CD reissue of the album, *Just Another Band from East L.A.* The eleven-song collection was made essentially for pocket change: $1,500 for studio time; $42 for 3,600 feet of tape; $700 for the mastering and pressing of 1,000 LPs; $750 for the manufacturing of jackets; $24 for two acetate test pressings; $30 for shrink-wrapping; and $200 for art and layout. Total cost: $3,246. (Torres maintains today that the finished album actually cost around $6,000—still virtually nothing for a finished LP.)

"We did things real cut-rate," says Torres. "For example, we rented a studio during, basically, downtime. The engineer we hired was working at a studio, and he knew that from midnight to six in the morning they weren't using it. So we gave them a couple of bucks, and we went in and used studio time when other people weren't using it. It was a matter of making sure that [Los Lobos] were real tight about what they were going to play, and we went in and recorded these things as efficiently as we could."

Just as the band members were autodidacts in the field of Mexican music, so Torres was in the realm of record production: "I had never produced a record. I had produced some music for little films, and I'd worked in radio, so I had some working knowledge of recording, a bit, but I didn't know how to make an album. Especially something such as this, where we had to do everything from start to finish—recording, mixing, and then actually pressing a record. So I went to the library and got some books—this is before the Internet, of course—and read up on how to produce a record."

Torres did receive some valuable assistance from Chris Strachwitz, an authority on Mexican folk and *conjunto* music whose El Cerrito, California–based label Arhoolie Records was a major repository of south-of-the-border roots styles.

"I called him up out of the blue," Torres recalls. "He didn't know who I was or anything. I said, 'Look, I know these guys. I think they're amazingly talented. In this bare-bones thing, we're going to try and make a record. Can I ask you a few questions?' He didn't know me from Adam, and he spent an hour on the phone with me, saying this is how you mic things, this is how you set things up ... He gave me specs on microphones. He suggested the kind of tape to use. He told me then a very elaborate story about how to actually press a record, and he gave the number of a small outfit in Alhambra, California, Virco Records. They did vanity records and stuff—high school marching bands and things like that. Strachwitz had some of his records pressed there.

"Chris Strachwitz was so helpful in this process, so generous, so selfless. Nothing in it for him—he just wanted to help some Chicanos down in L.A. put out a record."

Recorded live to four-track in guerrilla sessions at D&B Studios in Burbank and Associated Recorders in Hollywood, and mixed in one all-night stint at Gana Pali Studios on Hollywood

Boulevard, the eleven-track LP *Just Another Band from East L.A.* was a vinyl representation of Los Lobos' live repertoire, which at that time contained virtually no original material.

Rosas says, "[The songs] were all covers. We weren't writing too much. We wrote a couple of little things here and there, but not a whole lot . . . The only [original] thing [on the album] was an instrumental, 'Flor de Huevo,' that Dave had written. We used to play that. I think that was it. They were old songs, traditional songs."

Much of the material on the album obviously dated back to the earliest days of the band—three of the songs on *Just Another Band* can be heard in the concert filmed for L.A. public TV two years earlier. One of those numbers would have been familiar to nearly anyone on the East Side regardless of whether they'd heard of Los Lobos: the *bolero* "Sabor a Mi" had been a big local hit for El Chicano in 1971. The *son* "El Canelo" and the Bolivian folk tune "María Chuchena" were also holdovers, though the recorded versions obviously lacked González's harp on the former and doubled mandolin on the latter. By 1977, Rosas, the only fluent Spanish-speaking member of the group, had become the default lead singer; Hidalgo chips in a lead vocal on the uptempo section of the Mexican folk golden oldie "Cielito Lindo" and shares the lead on "María Chuchena," while on "Guantanamera," the inescapable Cuban song that dates back to the 1920s, Lozano takes his only lead vocal in the Lobos' history. Rosas claims that Lozano, who did not speak Spanish with any fluency, learned it phonetically.

The album, which served primarily as a souvenir of the band's shows, displays the economy of its creation and Torres's inexperience as a producer—some of the vocals could have benefited from additional takes, and Rosas slides woefully off pitch on "Sabor a Mi." But there's a real energy to the performances, plainly cut without overdubs. The playing is sound and dense, and Hidalgo's skill on violin and *requinto*—instruments he had only recently taken up—is especially impressive.

Released in early 1978 and known by early supporters as "the Yellow Album" for its monochrome cover, *Just Another Band from East L.A.* served its purpose: it got the music of Los Lobos del Este de Los Angeles into the hands of fans in the *barrio*.

"The guys would sell them at gigs," Torres recalls. "There was a [Music Plus] record store on Atlantic Boulevard in Monterey Park, on the border of East L.A. proper, [and] we sold them there, and they sold like crazy. They took them on a consignment deal. I made all these flyers, and we used to sell them through the mail. I had a post office box. I think [the LP cost] seven bucks, including shipping and handling. They'd tear off the bottom of a flyer, and they'd send them in. People would usually send in cash. I wrapped them myself and mailed them out. We sold a lot of records, hundreds and hundreds of records, that way."

After the first pressing sold out, the New Vista partners turned the masters over to the band. "They were very cool," says Rosas. "We paid them back, and that was it. We sold a lot of records off the back of our van. We sold it off the stage, and we had about ten record shops that were selling it for us. I think eventually we sold about eight thousand records. Little by little, year after year, we kept selling it."

It would be another ten years before Los Lobos made another full album of folk material, and then it would be under radically different commercial circumstances. Their music was about to take a sharp left turn stylistically and move from the East Side to points south, north, and west.

– 5 –

HAPPY HOUR

Going Electric at Las Lomas and
a Baptism of Fire at the Olympic

In late 1978, Los Lobos del Este de Los Angeles may have had an album to sell, but they found that they had fewer places to sell it. The institutional gigs that had been the band's bread and butter since the beginning of their career were beginning to disappear, thanks to draconian budget cuts in funding for the arts and education instituted by California's former governor Ronald Reagan, by then on his way to a run for the presidency.

Hidalgo says, "The funding that we used to make a living off of, playing all the schools, dried up, so we had to go to [playing in] restaurants. We had families by then, we had kids. We had to work."

"We had children, we had more responsibilities," Pérez adds. "We couldn't just depend on the weekend wedding gig or something. So we needed something real steady—if the wedding gig doesn't come in, nobody eats. So we had to resort to doing these restaurant gigs. We did a couple at the Red Onion chain."

The band members were doing what they could to make ends meet: Hidalgo and Pérez took work as instructors at Plaza de la Raza, the East L.A. center for arts and education, while Lozano worked as a teaching assistant at Hollenbeck Junior High in Boyle Heights. At one point around this time, jobs became so scarce that, at the behest of Mike Gonzalez, a former member of Rosas's band Fast Company, they worked as strolling musicians, in full *mariachi* garb, drumming up business for a new restaurant by performing Mexican tunes on the mall at the Music

Center in downtown L.A. A picture of the group from this era shows them looking stiff and distinctly uncomfortable in their matching embroidered black suits.

It was clear to the band members that supplementary employment was a must. And so Los Lobos fatefully took a regular job playing at Las Lomas, a restaurant in Anaheim Hills in Orange County, just east of Anaheim, the site of Disneyland.

"We became a hit there with the Mexican folk music," Rosas recalls. "They had two or three groups [playing there]. They had a traditional *mariachi* [band], there was us, and there was this group called Paul and Mike—they played country music. We came in with a little bit more traditional music. We would play for happy hour. We played like four hours a night—not every night, but we played several times a week. What happened was, even with the folk music, it started to become like a party."

The atmosphere in the restaurant, and the band's repertoire, began to mutate as the clientele at Las Lomas' bar began pitching requests at the musicians.

Rosas remembers that late in the evening, "things started settling down and the more serious drinkers started coming into the bar. The regulars would come just to see us. We were more exciting to them than the *mariachis*. Eventually, what happened was, we'd play a Mexican song, and it'd get quiet, and then somebody at the bar, a troublemaker, or a friend of ours, would say, 'Hey, man, you know [the Doors'] "Roadhouse Blues"?' or something.

"You understand, we come from a rock 'n' roll place, even though we're *folkloristas*. We knew our shit, though. We were rock 'n' roll kids. And any given moment, we could play a fuckin' Led Zeppelin song or whatever, but we weren't playing it. But we started one night. [Someone said,] 'Hey, man, play a Jimmy Reed song.' I did a Jimmy Reed song or something. That's how it started. 'Play a Rolling Stones song,' or, 'Play a Beatles song.' We started playing these songs acoustically. But it didn't jibe with the program. Here we were, hired to play Mexican music. Now we start playing Jimmy Reed songs or whatever, every once in a while. And the place went apeshit. People went, 'Fuck, man! You play *that*, too?' And we said, 'Yeah, we can play this.' And that's how it started—we were asked to play their favorite rock tunes, so we'd play 'em."

It was only a matter of time before the band began bringing electric instruments to Las Lomas.

"It just became a big party," says Hidalgo. "They had a drum set and amps, so I brought my nephew's Telecaster over one day."

"Eventually, Dave brought in a little Fender Princeton amp and put it in the corner and plugged in an electric guitar," Rosas recalls. "So here we are: I'm playing rhythm guitar, and Dave's playing electric guitar, and Louie's playing a snare and a cymbal. Then Conrad brings his electric bass in. Then eventually I brought an electric guitar."

It fell to Pérez, who probably hadn't touched a kit since his teens, to fill the drum chair in the newly electrified group.

"I played a little drums," he says. "Dave was actually a really good drummer, a really, really good drummer. [It may have been] his first instrument before he learned the guitar, because his brother was a drummer, too, and his other brother played guitar. There were musicians in the family. There were older brothers, and they were playing in bands. He played drums, I played drums. I was always around it. I wouldn't even call myself a drummer. But, if you fast-forward ten years, we needed one. And I was kinda the candidate.

"I say it as kind of a joke, but there's a lot to be said for showing up to rehearsal on time. If I'd showed up early, I'd have plugged in the guitar and said, 'I'm not going anywhere.'"

The band members agree that Los Lobos turned an important corner when Hidalgo took up the button accordion sometime in 1979.

"My brother-in-law's brother-in-law, Gus Leon, loved music," he says. "In the Montgomery Ward catalog, they used to sell older accordions, and he ordered the [Hohner] Corona II, the one that everybody uses for *norteño* music, and he had this project—'When I retire, I'm gonna learn how to play this thing.' I got to know him. I'd go over at my brother-in-law's house and hang out, and he pulled it out. I was messing around with it, and he said, 'Take it home and see what you can do with it.' So I started learning songs, and I'd go over to his house and play. Just before he was supposed to retire, he had a massive heart attack and passed away, so his wife gave me the accordion. She said, 'Keep it. He'd have wanted you to have it.' I didn't plan on playing accordion. But I ended up playing accordion."

Inspired by listening to the rocking accordion work of the Louisiana zydeco star Clifton Chenier and by the *norteño conjuntos* that could still be heard on Spanish-language radio stations in L.A., Hidalgo quickly showed the same facility on the squeezebox that he had on the exotic Mexican stringed instruments featured in the Lobos' folk sets. The Las Lomas sets began to include some Tex–Mex numbers, as well as a couple of songs associated with the '50s Chicano rocker Ritchie Valens.

"In a way, it was coming," Hidalgo says. "We'd gone as far as we could with Mexican music, to get to the core of it . . . We'd worked our way back to Thee Midniters, Cannibal and the Headhunters. We started seeing that it all made sense. There was a connection."

By the end of 1979, Los Lobos del Este de Los Angeles were performing for the first time as a full-blown rock 'n' roll band. But the evolution of their sound did not sit well with their employers at Las Lomas.

"People were getting into it," Lozano says. "They were partying. Pretty soon that place got really loud, and we ended up getting fired."

As the band slowly made their transition from folk to rock and continued to ply their trade on the East Side, its members dipped their toes into the roiling waters of L.A.'s punk rock scene, which had lifted off in earnest with the 1977 opening of the Masque, the music's first dedicated performance space, in Hollywood.

"We already knew about punk music and all of that shit," Rosas says. "We were fans of that stuff already. We were listening to some of that hardcore stuff [in the van] on the way to Las Lomas. We'd listen to a real hardcore Mexican folk song, and the next song would be the fuckin' Sex Pistols or the Cramps or something."

The musicians were also making their way over to Hollywood from the East Side to check out the new music firsthand.

"Our dear friend Eddie Zaragoza had a car," says Pérez. "I didn't drive, and Dave didn't drive then, either. Eddie was way into all the stuff that was happening, the scene out there. We would regularly take a trip with Eddie over to the Hollywood scene and check that out. We'd see the Plugz and the Rebel Rockers, all kinds of shit that was going on at the time. I think it was through Jesse Velo from Los Illegals that I met Tito Larriva."

Along with Alice Bag (née Alicia Armendariz), front woman of the Bags, and the members of the all-Chicano, Chula Vista–bred quartet the Zeros, Humberto "Tito" Larriva was one of the first prominent Latino performers on the L.A. punk scene. Born in Ciudad Juárez, Chihuahua, Larriva had arrived in L.A. in 1975. The singer–guitarist–actor (later featured as a heavy in several of director Robert Rodriguez's films) had founded the wound-up punk trio the Plugz, sometimes billed as Los Plugz, with Chicano drummer Charlie Quintana and Anglo bassist Barry McBride in 1978. That year, a three-track single by the band became the second release (following a 45 by the Germs) from Slash Records, the fledgling imprint of the like-named L.A. punk magazine. It prefaced the Plugz's self-released 1979 album *Electrify Me*, which included a high-velocity, lyrically retooled version of Ritchie Valens's "La Bamba."

It was Los Lobos' connection with Larriva that led to the group's first high-profile show outside of East L.A. In the spring of 1980, the Plugz were booked as an opening act on the first local performance by Public Image Ltd. (PiL), the confrontational British quartet fronted by John Lydon, theretofore better known as Johnny Rotten, lead vocalist of the notorious punk act the Sex Pistols. The date re-inaugurated concert events at the Olympic Auditorium, an ancient boxing and wrestling venue just south of the Santa Monica Freeway near downtown L.A., which had briefly served as a music venue in the late '60s.

After a local act called the .45s abandoned their slot as an opening act, Larriva called Pérez and asked if Los Lobos would be interested in appearing on the bill—but as an acoustic act performing their set of Mexican music.

"Tito was the culprit, and I was his co-conspirator, because I agreed to do it," Pérez says. "I never asked Tito if he in fact set us up. He called up and said, 'Hey, man, a band fell out, do you want to do this gig?' I don't know if he was on the other end of the phone, silently going, 'Hee hee!' But I said, 'Yeah, fine.'"

The Sex Pistols' first—and, at that point, last—U.S. tour in early 1978 had skipped Los Angeles; the nearest date (their final show before the group imploded) had taken place that January at the Winterland Ballroom in San Francisco, where audience members had demonstrated their affection by throwing everything they had in their possession at the stage. Los Lobos sensed what they could be in for opening for Johnny Rotten's first L.A. engagement—the PiL show was certain to attract the most aggressive element of the punk audience, who wanted to finally see English punk's greatest icon in person and could potentially stage a replay of the chaos at Winterland. Hidalgo says, "All these people who had missed the Sex Pistols, it was the next best thing for them."

"We knew that they threw shit, and they spit at people," Pérez says. "[We thought,] we're taking a big chance here, but we're just gonna do it." Rosas adds, "I told Tito, 'Are you sure, man? I know what the fuck's gonna happen—we're gonna go out there and it's gonna be a battle zone, man. Imagine a bunch of Mexicans playing fucking traditional music. They are gonna have a field day with us.'"

On May 4, 1980, I attended the PiL show at the Olympic as the critic for the local alternative weekly the *Los Angeles Reader*. I had never visited the fifty-five-year-old venue before, and it was a forbidding place. Fading photos of dimly recalled boxing luminaries lined its gray walls. Its floors were dark and sticky with the residue of several decades of spilled drinks. The air was thick with old smoke and violence.

Los Lobos del Este de Los Angeles—who had not been advertised as an opening act, owing to their late addition to the bill—took the stage clutching their acoustic instruments, bearded and long-haired, dressed in traditional Mexican *guayabera* shirts. The audience instantly reacted as one, and launched everything they had in their hands, and in their mouths, at the band.

Pérez remembers, "We went up onstage, and we went into the first couple notes of the first song, and I swear I could feel a rush of air come from the audience, from all of the middle fingers that went up at the same time. They were throwing shit like crazy. We didn't play a whole set, because by the time the serious projectiles started to fly, we booked. I don't know how many songs we did, maybe three, maybe four of 'em. Then we beat it. They started throwing real shit at us, and it hurt."

"The pennies and the dimes started coming in, and then the quarters started coming in," Rosas recalls. "And I remember they threw this big wad of wet paper, and it hit Dave in the face."

Lozano says with a laugh, "I was terrified. But we stood there, man. We fucking stood there. We said, 'Fuck this shit. Just keep doing it. Let's shove it down their throats.' So we did, man, until the bottles started flying. When the bottles started to fly, we said, 'OK, time to go!' Yeah, it was scary."

"Conrad was playing a *guitarron*," Pérez says, "and for months, maybe years after that show, it still had shit rattling around inside it that people had managed to [throw] into it."

My guest at the PiL show was a young saxophonist from Philadelphia who was beginning to make a name for himself as a sideman with a number of local punk bands. Recalling the gig later, Steve Berlin said, "I just remember the sort of weird Roman Coliseum–like vibe of that place. It seemed like the Christians and the lions, and they were the Christians. I remember them standing there somewhat impassively, just taking fusillade after fusillade of crap from the audience. Spit and bottles and cups."

By any measure, the PiL show was a catastrophe for the band, but they left the Olympic with a new resolve.

Says Pérez, "Because it was kind of a big deal for us, our wives came with us, and everyone in the family came, and they were all hanging out in the wings of the backstage area. We went around the curtain and went back. Our families were in tears. I had spit hanging from my chin. But of course, we had this adrenalin rush, because it was like being on a roller coaster or something.

"I suppose most people would have run back to East L.A. But no, we were kind of invigorated by it. We were taken aback a bit by the violence, and the formal rejection. But we didn't feel like we were beaten. We said, 'OK, let's move some shit around, and go back.'"

- 6 -

WOLVES OF HOLLYWOOD
Los Lobos' Arrival on the Punk Scene
and at the Whisky

In the wake of the Olympic confrontation, Los Lobos del Este de Los Angeles continued to scratch out a living playing weddings and parties on the East Side, but increasingly their attention was drawn to the Hollywood punk scene. It was as if they wanted to test themselves, and maybe test their hostile audience as well.

The band members continued to drive out of East L.A. to check out the local punk rock venues in Hollywood and beyond. They also got a chance to hear the latest developments on the punk side through the flood of singles and the occasional LP issuing from the city's many prolific independent record labels—Slash, Ruby, Bomp, Dangerhouse. It was only natural that Los Lobos would decide to make some DIY records of their own.

"OK, we've got to do this thing, and everybody was making their indie records," Pérez says. "All the homemade stuff was going on. So we just went and did it."

The two 45s that Los Lobos cut and released themselves in 1980–1981 offer a compact picture of the group at the very beginning of their rock incarnation. There isn't an original composition to be heard among the four songs they recorded, and the sound on most of them leans heavily on the border *conjunto* style they had adopted during their stay at Las Lomas.

The first single was tracked at Media Arts Studio in Hermosa Beach, south of L.A.; the label copy helpfully dates the session— October 9, 1980. The producer is identified as "Screwy Louie." The A side is a cover of "Under the Boardwalk," the Drifters'

1964 R&B ballad. David Hidalgo takes the soaring lead (his first solo vocal on record), effortlessly duplicating the tug of Johnny Moore's original performance. But the number receives a twist in the band's hands: in place of the lush string instrumental break on the Bert Berns–produced original, one hears a Tex–Mex button accordion solo. The flip was a rendering of "Volver, Volver," a *bolero* penned by Fernando Z. Maldonado that had been an enormous hit for the Mexican *ranchera* superstar Vicente Fernández in 1976. Returning to his original role as the group's ballad specialist, Cesar Rosas takes the lead vocal. Here the band offers an old-school East Side spin on the swaying, lushly romantic number, bringing some unidentified friends into the studio to scream and howl in the background, in the manner of the "live" supporting casts on Cannibal and the Headhunters' "Land of 1000 Dances" or the Premiers' "Farmer John."

The latter number appeared as the A side of the band's second single, probably recorded sometime in early 1981 at Sounds Good in West L.A. (Curiously, the band was billed on the first 45 simply as "Los Lobos" and on the second—and for the last time on record—as "Los Lobos del Este de Los Angeles.") It's a straightforward and rocking rendering, with a group vocal, of the old Don & Dewey tune, with its R&B roots expunged (as are the faux-party effects of the Premiers' version). The B side was again a tune in Spanish, written by Cesar Suedan and Guadalupe Trigo, a pair of professional songwriters from Mexico City, and first recorded by Los Alegres de Teran, a storied *norteño conjunto* whose career dated back to 1948. A lively two-step, the boastful "Anselma" would soon become a fixture of Los Lobos' live sets.

By the time Los Lobos recorded their calling-card 45s, punk rock had spread to the East Side, and had its own venue there: the Vex, a club run by beer distributor Joe Suquette (aka Joe Vex) and artist–musician Willie Herrón (of the band Los Illegals, which included the Lobos' friend Jesse Velo among its members) in an arts center on Brooklyn Avenue owned by the Roman Catholic archdiocese. The Hollywood punks would make pilgrimages to East L.A. to catch acts there, while the East Siders increasingly drove into Hollywood to check out the action there.

Los Lobos began plotting their incursion into Hollywood at an especially propitious time. By 1980, L.A. punk rock had become bifurcated. The first generation of punk acts had been supplanted to a degree by a newer, slightly younger group of bands, many of them bred in the beach communities to the south of L.A. and followed by younger, more pugnacious fans. The 1979 arrival of Hermosa Beach's Black Flag was the tectonic jolt that launched a wave of new hardcore punk acts—the Circle Jerks (which featured Black Flag's original lead singer, Keith Morris), T.S.O.L., Social Distortion, and many others. L.A. shows by these acts sometimes led to headline-grabbing, violent confrontations between their jacked-up fans and the local police.

In the words of Masque proprietor Brendan Mullen, many of the 1977–1978 punk generation "flopped the hardcore testo rage rite," and gravitated to a new breed of roots-based rock bands with a foot planted in the O.G. punk firmament. These included Top Jimmy and the Rhythm Pigs, a brawny, hard-drinking blues–rock unit fronted by "Top Jimmy" Koncek, a close friend of and sometime roadie for the punk band X; the Gun Club, a feral, unpredictable punk–blues unit led by vocal-ist–songwriter Jeffrey Lee Pierce, a blues devotee and frequent contributor to *Slash* magazine; and Phast Phreddie and Thee Precisions, a cranked-up R&B unit featuring singer Fred "Phast Phreddie" Patterson, former co-editor of *Back Door Man*, the first fanzine to explore L.A. punk. By late 1980, the NYC-by-way-of-Cleveland psychobilly quartet the Cramps had relocated to Los Angeles. The Flesh Eaters—one of the earliest L.A. punk bands, led by singer–songwriter Chris D. (born Chris Desjar-dins), another *Slash* contributor and head of the magazine's in-house subsidiary label, Ruby Records—would begin to probe punk–blues terrain with the 1981 album *A Minute to Pray, A Sec-ond to Die*, a swampy collection on which the bandleader was backed by members of X and the Blasters.

The Blasters proved to be the most prominent and popular

of these acts by far. Originally a quartet, the band was bred in Downey, just down the freeway from East L.A. In their teens, brothers Phil and Dave Alvin were bitten by the blues bug; they became habitués of the L.A. club the Ash Grove, where many of the best-known folk and electric blues performers played, and they sought out the local musicians who could teach them their craft, learning first-hand from such icons as Big Joe Turner, T-Bone Walker, and Little Richard's saxophonist Lee Allen (who would ultimately join the band in the '80s).

But the Blasters' style was multidimensional: they could play R&B, they loved country music, and they were also dyed-in-the-wool rockabilly fans who were initially embraced by the music's fervent L.A. cultists. Their debut album, 1980's *American Music*, was recorded in a Van Nuys garage by the Milan, Italy–born rockabilly fanatic Rockin' Ronnie Weiser, and released on his indie label Rollin' Rock Records, which also issued LPs by such first-generation rockabilly elders as Gene Vincent, Mac Curtis, Jackie Waukeen Cochran, and Ray Campi. By virtue of Phil Alvin's powerful, unmannered singing and Dave Alvin's adept guitar playing and original songwriting, the Blasters swiftly rose to the top of a pack of greasy local bands that also included Levi and the Rockats (a unit fronted by English singer Levi Dexter) and the Rockabilly Rebels (who frequently backed Ray Campi).

Los Lobos were early Blasters fans, and often listened to *American Music* in their van on the way to their own (still acoustic) gigs. Rosas says, "We loved their first record, man. We used to play the shit out of that record. Dave [Hidalgo] was the one who got a copy of it, and he put it on cassette."

"When we discovered the Blasters," Pérez remembers, "we said, 'Wow, here is a scene within a scene that we might fit into.'" Hidalgo adds, "We thought, if we're gonna get out of these restaurants, now is the time to give it a shot. The first Rollin' Rock Blasters record had come out. We heard that, and thought, 'Wow, man!' It blew my mind. 'What we're doing with the Tex–Mex and the Ritchie Valens stuff, it fits. Now, people are listening to different things.' That was why we made the push to get across the river."

The band could not have known that the Alvin brothers were already well aware of Los Lobos, and had been for more than five years, for they had seen the band's TV debut on *La Cultura* in 1975.

"The first time we had ever heard of them," says Dave Alvin, "Phil and I were at home, and we watched a thing on the local PBS station, channel 28. It was a half-hour documentary on this band from East L.A. that played traditional acoustic Mexican music from all of the various states."

Phil Alvin adds that the Lobos' example in fact had an impact on the genre-defying way in which the Blasters conceived of their own music: "I remember watching it and really being just impressed, particularly about the way they talked about Mexican music and the variety of it. When we went down to Rockin' Ronnie's and he kept pressuring us to say we played rockabilly and stuff like that, I remember thinking of those guys when I [told him] we played American music . . . I saw the affinities when I watched their PBS show. They were talking about all these various styles that they knew how to play and that they'd incorporate. I'd always felt the same myself [about American music]."

Thus it was probably inevitable that Los Lobos would approach the members of the Blasters and attempt to get their music to the more established band. Memories of their first meeting have dimmed over time: both the Alvins recall it taking place backstage after a show they played at the Whisky a Go Go on the Sunset Strip, while the Lobos remember it as happening at a date somewhere in the San Fernando Valley, possibly at the Country Club in Reseda.

Rosas says, "At the end of the show, Dave and Louie were walking out to the car in the parking lot, and Phil Alvin was walking right there next to them. Their cars weren't that far from each other. Everybody looked at each other. And I guess Dave and Louie said, 'Hey, man, we're fans. You guys were great tonight.' Then Phil does a double take. He says, 'Hey, where do I know you guys from? . . . Did you guys do a documentary or something?' You know how Phil is—he's a walking library. So Dave and Louie go, 'Yeah, we did do a documentary, way back, some years ago.' That's how the connection got made, right there."

Dave Alvin recalls, "We're looking at them, and because that TV show had made such an impression on us, it triggered this thing: 'Wait—are you *those guys?*' They were like, 'Yeah, yeah, yeah.' 'Oh, you're playing rock 'n' roll now.' 'No, we still do everything.'"

Los Lobos had come to the show with copies of their most recent 45 and a tape of their first original songs, recorded in Lozano's garage.

Rosas says, "I told the band, 'We gotta go back to the fucking garage, and we gotta start writing music.' We weren't writers. But I knew that that was very important, that we needed to do that. So we went back to the garage, and that's when we put together a handful of songs. Some of those songs were 'My Baby's Gone' and 'Let's Say Goodnight,' 'The Walking Song.' And some of those songs were on the demo we [gave to] the Blasters ... I had 'Why Do You Do,' a couple of other songs. Dave [Hidalgo] had a couple of songs."

Dave Alvin remembers that at their first encounter, "we were leaving town like the next day or two days later, and I remember being in the van, and we're driving ... 'OK, let's see what they sound like,' and we put [the tape] on. And it was like, 'OK, we're playing the Whisky, these guys are opening.'"

The initial encounter between the Blasters and Los Lobos must have taken place sometime in the fall of 1981, but it would in fact be some time before the Lobos would make their debut at the Whisky. Their first Hollywood booking came courtesy of a journalist and sometime promoter named Bill Bentley.

"We gave tapes to everybody," Dave Alvin says. "Bill was a Blasters supporter ... He was [music editor at] the *L.A. Weekly*, and Bill was involved loosely with [Tex–Mex rocker] Doug Sahm, and we thought, 'He's gonna like these guys.'"

According to Bentley's 2012 recollection in the *Weekly*, he offered the untested Chicano rockers $100 to open a date for Joe "King" Carrasco, the "Nuevo Wavo" singer–guitarist from Texas, at the Cathay de Grande, a onetime Chinese restaurant at Argyle and Selma in Hollywood whose dingy, low-ceilinged basement hosted most of the L.A. punk elite. A diary kept by Stella Aparicio, one of Los Lobos' devoted early fans, records the date as October 29, 1981.

Bentley—who would later serve for a decade as the band's publicist during their career at Slash and Warner Bros. Records—recalled in his story, "A dozen East L.A. friends had made the journey with them, dressed in their Sunday finest and full of a contagious celebration. The dancers filled the floor while the four musicians pushed their instruments into the red zone and, in front of their *amigos*, acted like they owned the room."

However, it was Los Lobos' debut date at the Whisky a Go Go, opening for the Blasters on January 24, 1982, which left a lasting impression on the Hollywood crowd. By that time the Downey group had been a potent draw for nearly two years, appealing to both hardcore rockabilly devotees and the sizable roots-oriented quadrant of the local punk contingent; their profile had been lifted by a series of ten West Coast dates opening for the British hard rock act Queen during the summer of 1980. The Blasters' self-titled debut album for Slash Records, released in late 1981, had just acquired national distribution from Warner Bros. Records, which had cut a deal with the punk-focused label. The collection was recorded by an expanded stage lineup in which the four original members—the Alvins, bassist John Bazz, and drummer Bill Bateman—were augmented by former Canned Heat and James Harman Band pianist Gene Taylor and two saxophonists, the group's mentor Lee Allen and the peripatetic Steve Berlin.

I was already a die-hard Blasters fan, and I was in the packed crowd that night at the Whisky. Like many others in the house, I was instantly intrigued and then enthralled by Los Lobos. The look of the band alone was alien, especially by the bizarre standards of L.A. punk: a quartet of bearded, mustachioed, long-haired young Chicanos clad in flannel shirts and denim. No set list from the show is known to exist, and I took no notes that evening, but it is safe to assume that Los Lobos performed Ritchie Valens's "Come On, Let's Go" and their Mexican standbys

"Anselma" and "Volver, Volver." One thing is certain: the group played loud, and they played fast.

Pérez told me later, "We didn't know what to expect. I guess somehow that PiL show was still on our minds, so when we went out onstage we were nervous, and the songs were a little faster than usual. I would say that fear definitely propelled us that night."

There had never been a band quite like that one playing in front of a punk-skewed crowd on a Hollywood stage, so Los Lobos' bow at the Whisky was something like a cultural experiment. But their energy was undeniable, and their mix of punk-style propulsion and rootsy authenticity flabbergasted the audience.

"I was curious about how the audience would react to them," Dave Alvin says. "It was [a] mixed [response], but not *bad* mixed. I think that there were a lot of people who were just confused. In general, though, I think people were floored."

"They just blew the place away," Steve Berlin said later. "Literally, overnight, everybody was talking about them, everybody was talking about how great they were, how this band with real vision and talent had sort of sprung up out of nowhere. It was like finding a tribe of Indians living under a freeway overpass. How could we have missed them? They were there the whole time."

Personally, I was impressed. During the course of Los Lobos' set, it slowly dawned on me that the group I was watching might be the same band of musicians who had so unforgettably gotten bottled off the stage at the Olympic for playing Mexican folk songs. My suspicions were confirmed by a conversation with Conrad Lozano in the Whisky's upstairs dressing room after the show.

I was astonished at how far Los Lobos had come in the short space of twenty months. I had no idea how far they would travel in the next two years.

– 7 –

ARRIVALS

Steve Berlin, Slash Records,
T Bone Burnett, and the Grammys

For the remainder of 1982, Los Lobos actively pursued more and more dates outside their East L.A. home turf.

A datebook kept by Stella Aparicio—whose brother Joel would go on to photograph the group extensively—reflects the Lobos' new territorial orientation. While they continued to play dates catering to their old audience—an opening shot for Tierra at the Roxy in West Hollywood, a Cinco de Mayo concert with Tierra and War, a September date at Belvedere Park in East L.A. commemorating Mexican Independence Day—the quartet focused its attention on dates in Hollywood.

There were few punk-oriented venues they didn't play. The Cathay de Grande became a mainstay, but they also performed at the Chinatown club Madame Wong's; the upscale Sunset Boulevard punk/roots watering hole Club Lingerie; the small, dumpy, comfortable West L.A. bar Club 88; and the larger, eclectic West Side outlet the Music Machine. Besides opening for such punk and roots attractions as the Blasters and the Plugz, they were billed with rockabilly performers like Rip Masters, James Intveld, and the Rebel Rockers, and with such other East L.A. invaders as Los Illegals and the Brat. They also made their first trip out of town as a rock group, traveling to Austin, Texas, for shows with Joe "King" Carrasco and Rank & File, the L.A./ Texas combine that would soon release their debut album on Slash; the latter, a country-skewed "cowpunk" group, featured brothers Chip and Tony Kinman of the early L.A. punk band the

Dils and Alejandro Escovedo, formerly the guitarist for the San Francisco punk act the Nuns.

To the Lobos' surprise, they found immediate acceptance among the punk and rockabilly audiences.

Pérez says, "We opened for the Blasters, and we blew everybody away, because they said, 'What the hell is this?' It was weird and strange enough for them to get their heads around, and eventually their arms around. We became good friends with a lot of these fans."

Rosas recalls that members of their old audience were taken aback: "The first couple of shows, we invited people from the East Side—sort of tough people, yet still conservative. They fucking got scared . . . People were deeply saddened by the step that we had taken. 'Oh, man, these guys are going downhill, and they're playing these places where there's nothing but death in the air. Guys are spitting at each other, and they've got shit through their noses.' They didn't understand it."

There was initially some sacrifice involved in playing to a Hollywood audience: the band members were looking at making considerably less money than they did on their home turf. "At that point we were playing every fucking thing that we could possibly do, man," Pérez says. "We would literally pass up a Saturday wedding for three hundred bucks to play the Cathay de Grande for forty bucks, and we'd have to chase [owner] Mike [Brennan] around the block to get it."

Rosas adds, "It got to be really weird, to go and play at the Cathay de Grande or something for free or a hundred bucks or seventy-five bucks or whatever it was . . . We'd come from making a living playing weddings and doing colleges and all that, to go to Hollywood and starve."

~~~~~~

At many of these early gigs, Los Lobos were augmented by another musician who started showing up at their shows, instrument in hand, just for the love of it: the Blasters' saxophonist Steve Berlin.

Born in Philadelphia, John Coltrane's longtime home base,

in 1955, Berlin was a hard-blowing, R&B- and jazz-savvy saxophonist who moved to L.A. at the age of twenty to work with members of a latter-day edition of the Soul Survivors, the Philly blue-eyed soul band whose single "Expressway to Your Heart" was the breakthrough hit for producers Kenny Gamble and Leon Huff in 1967. The quintet, known as the Beckmeier Brothers (fronted by guitarist Steve Beckmeier and his bass-playing sibling Freddie, who was then married to singer and future TV star Katey Sagal), was signed to Casablanca Records in 1977; their lone, self-titled 1979 release for the label included a single, "Rock and Roll Dancin'," which peaked at No. 59 on *Billboard's* Hot 100.

"We made a record, and it died a terrible death," Berlin says. "Right about the time that the band was falling apart was more or less when I started hanging out and doing the thing with Beachy."

In 1980, Steve broke in on the L.A. punk scene as the sax player with Beachy and the Beachnuts, a ramshackle unit fronted by sly punk soul man Bill "Beachy" White, which held down a regular weekend gig playing covers at Blackie's West on Main Street in Santa Monica, the tiny offshoot of a well-established punk venue in Hollywood. His association with the band, which essentially played the club for laughs and drinks, led to his first production credit: *Eleven It Ends*, a 1981 LP for Takoma Records (the L.A. indie label founded by guitarist John Fahey) by the Beachnuts' guitarist Brian Beverly.

The loose, free-swinging atmosphere at the Beachnuts shows led Berlin to pursue work with other L.A. punk bands. Initially his method was simple: He would show up at a club with his sax slung over his shoulder and ask to sit in. In a matter of months, he became the best-traveled and most in-demand saxophonist in the city; it was not unusual for him to play three shows in a night, driving all over town to play on a number or two.

By 1982, the mileage had paid off. Berlin had worked regularly with Top Jimmy & the Rhythm Pigs (playing on and producing the band's only album, *Piggus Drunkus Maximus*, belatedly issued in 1987), the Plugz (with whom he recorded the band's

1981 sophomore set, *Better Luck*), Phast Phreddie and Thee Precisions (as tenor saxophonist on Bomp's 1981 live album *West Hollywood Freeze-Out*), and the "all-star" iteration of the Flesh Eaters (on the 1981 Ruby/Slash album *A Minute to Pray, A Second to Die*). The latter unit included the Blasters' Dave Alvin. Berlin had signed on full-time with the Blasters in mid-'81, and, working side by side with the New Orleans sax legend Lee Allen, he recorded the albums *The Blasters* (1981) and *Non Fiction* (1983) and the live EP *Over There* (1982) with the group.

Although Berlin would continue to work full-time with the Blasters for more than a year, Dave Alvin says he knew as early as Los Lobos' first date opening for his band that his saxophonist was intrigued by the Chicano group.

"We did our soundcheck," he recalls, "and then they did their soundcheck, and Berlin went up and sat in with them at soundcheck. I turned to [Blasters road manager] Wally [Hanley] and said, 'Well, we just lost Berlin.'" (Hanley would himself later jump ship to work for Los Lobos.)

In short order, while maintaining his schedule with the Blasters, Berlin was also sitting in regularly with Los Lobos—sometimes playing with both bands on the same night at the dates they shared, at other times driving across town from a Lobos show to a Blasters gig. "I [was] going to extreme lengths [to play the Lobos gigs] because they were so much fun to play with," Berlin told me later.

~~~~~~~~~~~~~~~~~~~~~~~~~~~~~~~~~~~~~~~

As Los Lobos acquired a growing legion of followers with their shows, it became obvious to anyone paying attention that they would be the next L.A. act to make a record. The obvious outlet to release that record was Slash Records.

Operated by Bob Biggs, a UCLA grad and visual artist who had acquired control of *Slash* magazine from its original publisher, Steve Samiof, the Slash label had become in just a couple of years the most prominent independent punk label in the city, and one of the few to release more full-length LPs than singles. The imprint had been put on the map with the 1979 LP *(GI)* by the Germs, the most notorious of the first-generation local punk groups. That title had been succeeded by X's first two albums, *Los Angeles* and *Wild Gift* (the latter of which was named album of the year by the critics of the *Los Angeles Times*); the soundtrack for the wild, intimate 1980 L.A. punk documentary *The Decline of Western Civilization* (directed by Biggs's then wife, Penelope Spheeris); *The Blasters*; and *The Record*, the debut of the ultra-provocative, tongue-in-cheek quartet Fear. Chris D.'s Ruby subsidiary had issued *A Minute to Pray, A Second to Die* and the Gun Club's debut, *The Fire of Love*.

Slash was the natural destination for the much-talked-about Chicano quartet, and Los Lobos' supportive peers vocally campaigned for their signing.

Phil Alvin recalls, "Everybody was telling Bob Biggs, 'Get Lobos! Get Lobos!' I couldn't believe that he wasn't just jumping on it. I kept saying, 'For Christ's sake, you know, [sign them] for any reason—for the up-and-coming Mexican American market!'"

In March 1982, when the Blasters headed to New York for a series of local dates, the band took a stack of Los Lobos' "Farmer John"/"Anselma" single with them, going so far as to hand them out at the offices of Warner Bros. Records, which had just signed their distribution deal with Slash.

Says Dave Alvin, "We walked in and put on the Lobos tape. 'Sign these guys! You gotta sign these guys!' We were blasting the cassette through the Warner Bros. office in New York."

Biggs—who oversaw Slash's signings—initially was unmoved by the band. However, after being harangued by his acts, journalists, and local scenesters for the better part of a year, Biggs evidently connected all the dots at a club date on February 2, 1983.

"Finally," Pérez says, "Biggs came down to the show we did at the Roxy with Los Illegals. We opened for them; Biggs came, he heard our set, he heard two notes of Los Illegals, and he left. And then he said, 'OK, all right, let's do this.'"

"Everybody on that scene thought that they were amazing," Berlin adds, "but Bob Biggs thought that they were *trendy*. He sensed that it was something that was gonna go away. The only reason Biggs signed them was because, number one, no one would ever invite him to any more parties . . . My recollection is, he signed Lobos and [L.A. "Paisley Underground" band] Green on Red the same day, or the same moment. He thought that Green on Red was going to be the big deal, and that Lobos were never going to do anything."

It is a measure of how greatly Los Lobos were embraced by the L.A. rockabilly community that their first appearance as a rock band, after their own 45s, was on a compilation devoted to local acts in the genre.

L.A. Rockabilly was a Rhino Records collection assembled by Art Fein, the Blasters' original manager. The participants included Dave Alvin, X's rockabilly-schooled lead guitarist Billy Zoom, Jerry Sikorski of the Rockabilly Rebels, and Orange County rockabilly rulers the Paladins. Nestled among the tracks was Los Lobos' "We're Gonna Rock." Betraying its low recording budget, this seemingly one-take wonder, already a fixture of the band's club sets, was a Cesar Rosas original; the execution is messy, but its blinding speed, high energy, and snapping solos by Rosas and Hidalgo conjure the live excitement the band was capable of generating in their early days.

"We're Gonna Rock" was produced by Steve Berlin, who continued to play regularly with the Lobos and entertained serious ambitions about producing them. "I was sort of hanging around Slash at that time," he says. "Everybody at Slash knew that I wanted to produce records."

Nonetheless, Slash and Warner Bros. asked the Lobos to vet a short list of more experienced prospective producers. One of them was actually a Warner Bros. act, a singer–songwriter named T Bone Burnett.

Rosas remembers, "I really didn't know too much about T Bone, although they told me who he was, that he had played with Bob Dylan back then, and that he was a producer. There was a handful of producers that most of us went to interview. That one particular day, it was just myself and Conrad who went and talked to T Bone. He was doing a session over at [Hollywood studio] Ocean Way. He invited us down there . . . We went in there and talked to him. He actually played us some of the stuff he was doing, and we were pretty impressed."

At that point, T Bone Burnett had not yet become *T Bone Burnett!*—thirteen-time Grammy winner; producer of two Album of the Year Grammy winners (the multiplatinum soundtrack for the Coen Brothers' 2000 period comedy *O Brother, Where Art Thou?* and Robert Plant and Alison Krauss's 2007 collaboration *Raising Sand*); go-to music producer for features like the 2005 Johnny Cash biopic *Walk the Line* and TV shows like *Nashville*; Oscar, Grammy, and Golden Globe–winning co-writer of "The Weary Kind" for the 2010 feature *Crazy Heart*. In early 1983, Burnett was just a well-traveled journeyman musician with plenty of interesting credits but an as-yet-unfulfilled career.

Born Joseph Henry Burnett and raised in Fort Worth, Texas, Burnett was barely out of his teens when he produced "Paralyzed," a single by the eccentric Lubbock-born performer Norman Odam, who had rechristened himself the Legendary Stardust Cowboy; the independent 45, on which "the Ledge" yammered incomprehensibly and blew a bugle solo over Burnett's manic drumming, became a regional hit, was picked up for national distribution by Mercury Records, and landed Odam a chaotic 1969 appearance, as "the discovery of the week," on *Rowan & Martin's Laugh-In*.

Burnett's own 1972 album, *The B-52 Band & the Fabulous Skylarks*, went nowhere, but his friendship with Bob Dylan's aide-de-camp Bob Neuwirth landed him work with Dylan's star-studded, carnival-like Rolling Thunder Revue tour of 1975–1976. With two tour mates, multi-instrumentalist David Mansfield and singer–guitarist Steven Soles, Burnett formed the left-of-center rock group the Alpha Band, which released a trio of critically well-received but commercially unsuccessful LPs on Arista Records in 1977–1978.

Based in L.A. in the early '80s, Burnett finally began to hit his stride as a solo artist. In 1980—the same year he and Mansfield appeared in director Michael Cimino's costly, catastrophically received Western *Heaven's Gate*—he released the roots-based album *Truth Decay* on Takoma Records (the same imprint that had issued the Steve Berlin–produced Brian Beverly album). Written during months stuck on Cimino's locations in Montana, the record attracted attention by mating Burnett's caustic humor and spiritual concerns to rockabilly, R&B, and Tex–Mex settings. He subsequently acquired something of an underground following among local critics with weekly appearances at Hop Sing's, a club in the West L.A. community of Venice. Signed to Warner Bros., he released a six-song EP, *Trap Door*, in 1982; he was working on his first full-length album for the label, to be titled *Proof through the Night*, at Ocean Way in 1983.

Burnett recalls that Warner Bros. vice president of A&R Steven Baker asked him to see one of the Lobos' local shows, and he dropped by a date at the Cathay de Grande to check them out.

"They were a groove," Burnett says. "They were the killingest band in town at that point. They probably still are . . . With David Hidalgo, you knew immediately that this was one of the most amazing guitarists, musicians, ever. That was not hard to tell. Cesar was such a bad, bad man. The whole band was great. Louie's a killer writer."

As a Texan, Burnett was also thoroughly familiar with the Tex–Mex music Los Lobos were mining, and he notes that it had played a role in his own work as well: "Trio San Antone was a favorite of mine, and I think theirs, too, and [Tex–Mex accordionist] Flaco Jimenez and all that. They played that *norteño* music beautifully, and I love that music. And I loved Buddy Holly, who played Texas–Mexican music. There was a lot of that stuff down there. They understood all that. They understood all the connections, how it all made sense."

Burnett was formally brought on board to produce, with Berlin on hand as an instrumental contributor and, ultimately, as co-producer.

"As I remember it," Burnett says, "I started out as the producer, and he wasn't a member of the band and he wanted to be a part of it, but I was happy to include him as producer, so I brought him in as producer on the EP."

The saxophonist was not yet officially a member of Los Lobos when the sessions started, but it appeared inevitable that he would soon join the group.

Pérez says of Berlin, "He started hanging out with us when we were playing the scene at Madame Wong's and all those joints. When the first record happened, that's when we said, 'Wait a second, I guess you're in the band now.' That was it. We didn't have to put out a classified ad for a sax player. He just started showing up."

"By that time," Berlin says, "I'd been playing with them enough that I was integral—the sax parts were built into some of the songs—not all of them, but 'Let's Say Goodnight,' 'Anselma.' . . . When I started the record I was in the Blasters. By the end of the record I was in Los Lobos."

Distributing label Warner Bros. was very much in the driver's seat in terms of how Los Lobos would be launched as a recording act, and the company determined that the group's first release on Slash would be an extended-play record, or EP, not a full album.

Pérez says, "They gave us an EP. Green on Red got a full record. They gave us an EP because I think they weren't sure—'I don't know about these guys.'" However, Burnett, whose own initial release for the label had been an EP, disputes this notion, and believes that, like him, the Lobos were part of an ongoing marketing experiment: "[Warner Bros.] had just done that EP with me, and they wanted to try and get into EPs. That was something they were up to at the time."

Recorded over the course of two weeks at Warner-owned Amigo Studios in North Hollywood, the seven-song, nineteen-minute EP, titled . . . *and a time to dance*, is a crisply recorded representative chunk of Los Lobos' early Hollywood club set, recorded by musicians who were still finding their footing as songwriters but already flexing a distinctive and lively sound of their own.

"We thought there was obviously a need to write, first of all," Rosas says. "The second thing was, well, what do we start writing about? So we started writing about stuff that felt good, which during that time was roots music. We were listening to R&B, and we liked zydeco music. We were listening to that during those years, and we started writing along those lines."

The record contained four original songs—Pérez and Hidalgo's "Let's Say Goodnight," "Walking Song," and "How Much Can I Do?" and Rosas's "Why Do You Do." All of them were simple narratives of romantic discord, and they're more interesting as signposts of Los Lobos' musical development than as compositions of any great lyrical distinction. In particular, "Let's Say Goodnight" and "Walking Song" reflect Hidalgo's virtuosity on accordion and lead guitar, respectively, while "Why Do You Do," an old-school rock-bopper, lays down the basic framework for Rosas's writing in the immediate years to come. Steve Berlin is already wholly integrated in the band's overall sound, alternately offering tight unison lines with the guitarists and surging solo work.

The three covers reiterated Los Lobos' Chicano roots. The album-closing "Ay Te Dejo En San Antonio" is a faithful rendering of an old *ranchera* by *conjunto* godfather Santiago Jimenez, an early master of the border-style accordion and father of Flaco Jimenez. "Come On, Let's Go" is a de rigueur cover of Ritchie Valens's first single from 1958, a crowd-pleasing staple of the band's repertoire since their Las Lomas days. The jewel of the EP is a re-recorded version of "Anselma," the B side of the band's 1981 single. The song, a consistent house-shaker at the Lobos' club shows, now found Berlin doubling Hidalgo's accordion part. Even if English-speaking listeners couldn't understand the Spanish narrative—a tough-guy suitor's threat to disrupt his sweetheart's marriage to another man by any means necessary—they would be carried away by the song's leaping energy.

Released in September 1983, . . . *and a time to dance* made something of a splash nationally by virtue of its sheer novelty. It garnered almost universally positive reviews, and, in February 1984, it was honored as the best EP of the year by participating critics in the *Village Voice*'s annual Pazz & Jop critics poll, which tallied ballots from 207 national writers that year.

As an EP, the record had little chance of making much of a commercial impact on a national level, and it failed to even dent *Billboard*'s Top 200 Albums chart. However, . . . *and a time to dance* notched a more important artistic impression early the next year.

In 1984, the National Academy of Recording Arts and Sciences rewarded Michael Jackson at the Grammy Awards for the record-breaking sales of his *Thriller* with an equally record-setting eight trophies. A then-record 43.8 million people tuned in to CBS to watch the ceremony, beamed live on February 28 from the Shrine Auditorium in L.A. That year, the Academy instituted the brand-new category of Best Mexican American Recording. While winners in the major categories were announced during the network broadcast, awards in smaller, niche categories, revealed earlier in the day, were briefly flashed on-screen during the course of the televised show.

The night of the Grammys, Los Lobos were 1,895 miles from home, in New Orleans, in the middle of their first tour of the East and Southeast, driving from gig to gig in a van and sharing a single hotel room on the road. They were to play Jimmy's Music Club that night, but repaired to a local bar to watch the awards show on TV before their set.

Berlin recalls, "[The announcer] said, 'Earlier this evening, these awards were handed out.' And sure enough, there's a picture of Los Lobos. So we start flipping out—'Oh, shit, we won this thing! We won a Grammy!' And this old drunk at the bar said, 'Yeah, *right*, buddy.' We were all ecstatic. And we get to the gig, and there's five people there."

- 8 -

QUANTUM LEAP
How Will the Wolf Survive?

Thanks to the terms of Warner Bros. Records' distribution deal with Slash Records, Los Lobos essentially became Warner Bros. artists not long after the band's surprising Grammy win.

Steve Berlin recalls, "When Slash connected with Warner Bros., as I understood it, the deal was that at Warner's will, they could upstream something they liked from the Slash catalog into the Warner's system. Not long after the EP was released and won the Grammy, we were upstreamed into Warner's."

While Bob Biggs and the other Slash staffers were still deeply involved with the group, the band would henceforth enjoy the greater marketing, promotion, and publicity clout of the major label, and would be in much closer contact with Warner executives—most importantly, in terms of their future, with the label's head of A&R, Lenny Waronker.

Though Los Lobos' star was plainly on the rise, they primarily remained hometown heroes at the beginning of 1984. A compelling video snapshot of the band, broadcast locally just as they were taking off early that year, can be found on YouTube.

Titled . . . *And a Time to Dance*, director Sylvia Morales's half-hour film was shot over the course of several months in 1983 and aired in May 1984 as part of another Latino-oriented series, *Presenté*, on L.A.'s PBS outlet, KCET. The band is seen recording "Anselma" with T Bone Burnett and engineer Mark Linett, rehearsing in a garage, and performing at this writer's wedding (one of the last they would play). The majority of the program was filmed at an invitational Club Lingerie show in November 1983. No longer bearded (save Cesar Rosas, who is rocking his Chicano hipster shades-and-goatee look) or long-haired, onstage the band looks tidy and New Wave–slick in vintage togs procured for the occasion. The rockers heard live on the show are taken at killing punk tempos, while the Tex–Mex songs bound along energetically, driving the audience to dance en masse in a huge circle, their arms linked. Appropriately, the telecast ends with "Let's Say Goodnight"; under the credits, David Hidalgo shows off some new skills, playing the steel guitar on a cover of Santo & Johnny's dreamy 1959 instrumental hit "Sleep Walk."

It's a performance typical of that time—tight, ferociously energetic, musically diverse, crowd-pleasing. The only thing missing: truly distinctive new songs. The lone unrecorded tune that would have been unfamiliar to a Los Lobos fan tuning in to *Presenté* was "Corrido #1"; not really a *corrido* in the storytelling sense, but rather a love song (penned by Rosas and sung in duet with Lozano) cast as border two-step, it was a perfectly engaging and satisfying number which nonetheless didn't extend the boundaries of the group's music.

With the recording of their first full-length album for Slash/Warner's now pending and a growing national reputation to live up to, Los Lobos had to improve their game as songwriters. Though the group had been in business for over a decade, they had released just five original songs—four on . . . *and a time to dance*, plus "We're Gonna Rock" on the *L.A. Rockabilly* compilation.

"We knew that we had to dig deeper," Hidalgo says. "We had to step it up a little bit. We were in a position to say something, and we figured we had to give it a shot."

Both Rosas and the team of Pérez and Hidalgo—who had been writing together since they were in high school—had brought material to the table for their debut Slash EP. But all that work had operated within fairly narrow genre confines, and Hidalgo and Pérez now looked to the writing of Dave Alvin of the Blasters as a model. By the time Los Lobos began work on their album,

Alvin had already crafted a number of sharply penned, novelistic songs—"Border Radio," "Bus Station," "Long White Cadillac," "Red Rose"—for his own band's two Slash albums.

"Dave's writing was a big influence on us," Hidalgo says. "What we loved about Dave's writing is that it was so clean and to-the-point . . . His style was never too flowery. It was always right. It was a storytelling kind of thing. 'I love you, baby'—there's room for that, but to have a song tell a story, create a vision, that's where that came from."

Hidalgo also acknowledges a number of other songsmiths whose example played into the team's work at that point: bluesmen Willie Dixon (the principal songwriter for Chicago's Chess Records in the '50s and '60s) and Jimmy Reed, country's Hank Williams and Merle Haggard, English folk–rocker Richard Thompson (a favorite of Hidalgo and Pérez since his work with Fairport Convention in the late '60s), and Los Lobos' '80s contemporaries Elvis Costello and Nick Lowe.

A good portion of the new album grew out of work during the sessions, according to Burnett: "They wrote in the studio quite a bit. We went in with less than an album's worth of material . . . We would record something that didn't have the lyrics yet, and David and Cesar would almost scat over them. They would just sing a melody over the band [track], and then they would go home and write lyrics.

"That happened two or three times during that period of time. Two or three of the songs were done that way. Maybe they had a verse and a chorus. We would go ahead and record it because we had the studio time, and then they would finish it off. We used to work a lot longer on things than we do these days."

Pérez and Hidalgo's deeper concentration on writing bore fruit in important songs that marked a gigantic stride beyond the material found on the band's debut EP.

"'A Matter of Time' was a big breakthrough," says Hidalgo. "It was a big step, and it helped pave the way." The song, which ultimately appeared as the second track on the band's major label debut LP, immediately commanded the listener's attention. Cast as a dialogue, the hushed number depicts a farewell between a

Mexican laborer, leaving to cross the U.S. border in search of possibly illusory work, and his uncertain wife. Painted with focused economy, the song unfolds like a brilliantly told short story:

> *Speak softly, don't wake the baby*
> *Come and hold me once more before I have to leave*
> *'Cause there's a lot of work out there, everything will be fine*
> *And I'll send for you, baby, it's just a matter of time*
>
> *Our life, the only thing we know*
> *Come and tell me once more before you have to go*
> *That there's a better world out there, though it don't*
> * feel right*
> *Will it be like I hope? It's just a matter of time*

For the first time, Los Lobos were writing about the fabric of their own people's difficult experience, not as any sort of political broadside, but with artfulness, a fine-tuned clarity, and powerful emotional affect. And, like most great songs, it retained its potency over time.

Burnett, who was returning as Los Lobos' co-producer with Steve Berlin, notes, "'A Matter of Time'—look at how important that song is today. It's *still* a matter of time—there are people who have been waiting for their families for thirty years."

Another Hidalgo–Pérez composition, the up-tempo "Will the Wolf Survive?" could stand as a metaphorical complement to "A Matter of Time":

> *Through the chill of winter, running across a frozen lake*
> *Hunters out on his trail, all odds are against him*
> *With a family to provide for, the one thing he must*
> * keep alive*
> *Will the wolf survive?*

Hidalgo says that Dave Alvin supplied the direct inspiration for "Wolf": "He told us, 'You need an anthem. "American Music," that's our anthem.' That kind of spurred the idea."

He explained the genesis of the song to me in 1985: "Louie was looking through a *National Geographic* and found the article 'How Will the Wolf Survive?' And he flipped the page, and there was another story that fit right in with it. There was a picture of this gaunt old guy who was hitchhiking on the highway with his dog. There it was."

As these new songs began to materialize, it became apparent to the band's producers that something new was afoot in Los Lobos' music.

Berlin says, "I remember very, very distinctly when Dave started singing ['Will the Wolf Survive?'] for the first time that the thought entered my head: 'OK, everything is different from this point forward.' Everything we had done up 'til 'Wolf' was our version of something else they had done or something they had taken with them. In everything prior to 'Wolf,' our influences were pretty obviously on our sleeves. I would say that 'Wolf' was the first song where we had built something out of those influences that was uniquely ours. It was just us being us. It was pretty obvious that it was special. We didn't have anything that was as obviously unique as that song."

"[Previously] they'd been way more into a 'Don't Worry Baby' kind of mode, more of a blues kind of mode," Burnett says. "I had thought for a long time that the Hispanics were the new soul men. There was a sense that there was something coming from the Hispanic community that was going to be unbelievably soulful. When they showed up, I thought, 'OK, this is *them*—these are the ones.' They just told the truth, but it was in the way that a blues musician would tell the truth. But when they started getting into those high-consciousness songs, as I'd call them, they started telling the truth at a different level."

When Los Lobos' first full-length album, *How Will the Wolf Survive?* (the title of which would spawn a thousand unimaginative newspaper and magazine headlines), was released on October 29, 1984, the band's devoted followers understood immediately that some sort of quantum leap had taken place. While the group continued to draw water from the same roots-music well that had nourished their sound to date, all the elements were arranged and deployed with a new assurance and a fresh intelligence.

Beyond the striking "Will the Wolf Survive?" and "A Matter of Time," the album contained other keenly crafted new compositions. "Don't Worry Baby," credited to Rosas, Pérez, and Burnett, was a surefire house-rocker sporting short, tough blues guitar solos by Rosas and Hidalgo. Rosas's solo composition "I Got to Let You Know" was a compelling R&B-cum-*norteño* strut, while "Corrido No. 1" remained the same bouncy Tex–Mex polka that had been moving crowds around on the Lobos' dance floors for awhile. For Hidalgo and Pérez's part, "Evangeline," a skillful narrative cameo about a footloose teen runaway, almost rose to the level of their best work on the album; by comparison, the bopping "Our Last Night" (graced with some countrified steel guitar playing by Hidalgo, in one of his rare recorded forays on the instrument) and the sinuous hip-shaker "The Breakdown," while rhythmically pleasing, broke no new lyrical ground yet still engaged the ears and the feet. The album was filled out with a faithful, ripping cover of "I Got Loaded," a slice of swampy R&B celebrating the joys of alcoholism originally cut by Little Bob & the Lollipops on the La Louisianne label in 1965; the self-referential, time-shifting traditional number "Serenata Norteña," performed *en Español* with *conjunto* instruments; and "Lil' King of Everything," a brief Pérez–Hidalgo instrumental that served as an introduction to the album-closing "Will the Wolf Survive?"

In an era before social media, when the music press still directed the serious discussion of music, *How Will the Wolf Survive?* arrived as a revelation. Some critics who may have considered Los Lobos some sort of aberrant Chicano cover band now welcomed the group's expansive new music with surprised adulation.

Robert Christgau, the highly opinionated and notoriously difficult-to-please music editor and lead critic of the New York alternative weekly the *Village Voice*, awarded the album a much-prized "A" grade in his "Consumer Guide" to current recordings. He pithily summarized the record's achievements: "Where their EP was a straightforward account of a world-class bar band in command of what we'll call Chicano R&B, a relatively specialized indigenous style with unexploited mass potential, their debut LP makes it sound as if they invented the style. Who did the original of that one, you wonder, only to discover that you're listening to the original. Listen a little more and you figure out that these slices of dance music have lyrics, lyrics rooted in an oppression the artists really know about—the love songs return incessantly to the separation that defines migrant laborers' lives."

Many in the rock-crit constituency echoed Christgau's sentiments. When the *Voice*'s annual Pazz & Jop critics poll appeared in early 1985, *How Will the Wolf Survive?* was named the No. 3 album of 1984, appearing on the ballots of 102 of the poll's 240 contributing writers. It was in heady company that year: the LP was surpassed in the tally by two of the zeitgeist-defining releases of the time, Bruce Springsteen's *Born in the U.S.A.* and Prince and the Revolution's *Purple Rain. Rolling Stone* named the group band of the year and best new artist in its own critics poll.

Despite largely rapturous reviews, *How Will the Wolf Survive?* was not a hit. It failed to spawn a Top 40 single, and, while it spent thirty-four weeks on *Billboard*'s album chart, it never rose higher than No. 47. Nonetheless, in 1985 the band was able to parlay the record's exceptional press and the afterglow of their Grammy win into a busy year of touring that took them to Japan for the first time. At home, amid a run of headlining club and theater shows in the United States, they played L.A.'s Greek Theatre for the first time in July.

– 9 –

BREAKDOWNS

The *Graceland* Session and
By the Light of the Moon

It is a measure of Los Lobos' burgeoning artistic cachet that they were asked during the summer of 1985 to collaborate with one of the most popular and respected American singer–songwriters, their Warner Bros. labelmate Paul Simon.

Through the late '60s and early '70s, Simon had forged an estimable commercial track record in Simon & Garfunkel, his vocal duo with Art Garfunkel; they had released five multiplatinum studio albums, and Simon had penned such enduring classics as "The Sounds of Silence," "Mrs. Robinson," and "Bridge over Troubled Water." Simon's solo records for Columbia following the pair's 1971 split were also highly esteemed, and all reached either platinum or gold status. However, his fortunes had experienced a serious downturn after he signed with Warner Bros. in 1980: the soundtrack for his flop movie vehicle *One-Trick Pony* had been a comparative failure despite its Top 10 single "Late in the Evening," and his 1983 studio album *Hearts and Bones* had enjoyed neither critical acclaim nor chart success, peaking at No. 35, the lowest ebb of his career to date.

Steve Berlin, then an avowed Simon fan, says, "At that time, Paul—who I respected and still respect as one of the finest American songwriters alive—had had a couple of stiffs. *Hearts and Bones* did like next to nothing. My perception of the moment was, here's this great American songwriter who's on a slight dip in his career. So Lenny [Waronker] came to us and asked if we would participate in this record that he was doing . . . As a favor to Lenny, and it was kind of a big deal to me, we agreed to go in the studio with Paul, and Lenny said, 'Just see what happens.' We weren't promised anything; we didn't promise him anything. We didn't know what was gonna go down. The way it was put to us was, 'We'll jam.' 'All right, we'll jam.'"

At the first day of sessions at Warner's Amigo facility, Simon played some of the other music he had recorded for the members of Los Lobos. Still in raw form, and lacking lyrics, the material moved dramatically away from the folk-based style of his early work. The L.A. act's sound meshed with what they heard, for, like their *norteño*-style material, the tracks Simon had cut were made with accordion-based units—the Louisiana zydeco group Rockin' Dopsie & the Cajun Twisters and some South African bands that also made prominent use of the instrument.

Work in the studio became an instantly uncomfortable chore, for, Berlin says, Simon and his longtime engineer Roy Halee were "just really bizarre dudes" who mainly kept themselves walled behind the glass in the control room, while Los Lobos—never a jam-oriented group to begin with—were uncertain about what they were being asked to do out on the floor.

Berlin says, "There wasn't anything close to clicking, even vaguely close to an idea. We'd noodle on something, and Paul would go, 'Nah, I don't like that, let's try something else.' We'd go on to something. 'Nah, I don't like that, let's try something else.' It went on and on and on and on and on ... [And Simon] had zero musical input. He did not come up with a chord, not a melody, not a sequence, not a note."

Before the end of the day, the band was on the phone with Waronker, pleading to be liberated from the session. However, the A&R exec succeeded in convincing them to go in for another day of work with Simon. It was at that point that David Hidalgo pulled out a half-developed musical sketch that attracted Simon's attention.

"Dave started playing the song that became 'The Myth of Fingerprints.'" Berlin says. "It was a song—I don't think we'd ever rehearsed it, but it was just a little riff ... But Paul goes, 'Hey, what's that?' We said, 'Oh, that's a song we've started work on for the next record.' He goes, 'Well, can we use that?' We said, 'Fuck, yeah.' Finally we had something that sounded like something. We played it, and at that point it clicked, I guess. We ran it through a couple of times, and we got something that was close enough, and then we literally could not get out of that fucking studio fast enough."

Hidalgo and Rosas later returned to the studio for vocal overdubs, and Louie Pérez's original drum track was replaced with work by top studio musician Steve Gadd. The arduous session remained an unpleasant yet happily distant memory until September 1986, when Simon's album—now known as *Graceland*, and mainly comprising songs developed from his work with the South African musicians—was released to great critical acclaim and astonishing commercial success. The African performers were in many cases given co-songwriting credit. However, Los Lobos' number, called "All Around the World or the Myth of Fingerprints," was credited, "Words and music by Paul Simon."

"We said, 'Well, obviously that's somebody's mistake,'" Berlin says. "So we started calling. [The band's manager] Linda [Clark] called Paul's people, and said, 'Hey, you can fix this, right?' Silence. No response. This went on for a long time—no response, no response, no response. We didn't think anything of it, because in our heads it was just a silly mistake that somebody had made. Because, very, very clearly, [Simon] had nothing whatsoever to do with the music as far as we were concerned. This went on for awhile. Days go by, and weeks go by. Finally, the response from Paul, directly from Paul, given to us, was, 'Hey, you don't like it, sue me. See what happens.' That was the end of the conversation . . . Since there were no contracts signed, there was no way to prove that that song had ever been played before the day in the studio, and we were sort of out of legal options."

Los Lobos may have later savored the accusations of cultural imperialism that were leveled at Simon at the time of the album's release for his work with the South African musicians, and criticism of his violation of the UN's cultural boycott of South Africa, then still governed under the specter of apartheid. But you can't take a sense of ethical superiority to the bank. Los

Lobos never derived a penny of songwriting royalties from their work on *Graceland,* which was ultimately certified for sales of five million copies in the United States and has reportedly sold fourteen million copies worldwide. In fact, the band has been virtually written out of the history of the album, which won the Album of the Year Grammy in 1987; they are barely acknowledged in the lavish four-disc twenty-fifth-anniversary boxed set edition of the album issued in 2012.

Through a spokesperson at Sony Music's Legacy Recordings division—which currently controls all of Paul Simon's catalog, including *Graceland*—Simon declined a request to be interviewed for this book.

Los Lobos had weightier things than dueling with a pop star on their minds in 1986. Much of the year was occupied with the recording of a follow-up to *How Will the Wolf Survive?* with Berlin and T Bone Burnett returning to co-produce. Again, the band sought to up the ante artistically.

Hidalgo says, "We were trying to take it somewhere else—a step further or something, just to not repeat what we'd done. The storytelling style of writing went even further on that album, I think."

If anything, the album—titled *By the Light of the Moon* and ultimately released on January 19, 1987, a little over two years after *How Will the Wolf Survive?*—exhibited an even greater extension of Los Lobos' talents beyond the preceding album than *Wolf* had beyond the debut EP. Save one number, the lachrymose traditional *bolero* "Prenda Del Alma," all of the LP's tracks were original songs, and they were stunning in their depth, and in their darkness.

By the Light of the Moon is one of the quintessential albums of the Reagan era in America. Issued in the middle of President Ronald Reagan's second term in office, it reflects the oppressive mood that had settled on the citizenry. The record's very title—drawn from a lyric ("Tear-stained faces by the light of the moon") in one of its songs, "River of Fools"—seemed an overt reference to the 1984 Reagan campaign's celebrated TV ad promising "morning again in America." "One Time One Night," the pessimistic Hidalgo–Pérez song that led off the collection—a catalog of murder, kidnapping, and sudden, inexplicable death "one time one night in America"—gave the lie to the Reagan administration's bright, hollow vision for the country.

Coming from a group that had only recently been considered merely the purveyors of appealing, danceable roots–rock, the bleakness of many of the new numbers came as something of a shock. Some of Hidalgo and Pérez's songs were intimate, caustic depictions of their characters' errant romantic lives ("The Hardest Time," "All I Wanted to Do Was Dance," "Is This All There Is?"), while others were sprawling, appalled takes of a world spinning out of control with violence, war, and chaos ("One Time One Night," "The Mess We're In"). Even Rosas's bluesy material, reliably rousing and cheerful in the past, took on somber undercurrents: "My Baby's Gone" was a simple howl of pain, "Shakin' Shakin' Shakes" anticipated an apocalyptic quake along L.A.'s long fault lines, and even the sprightly, rhythmic, Motown-derived "Set Me Free (Rosa Lee)," with a screaming Junior Walker–like sax break by Steve, lyrically lamented the disappearance of real-life East Side haunts—Brooklyn Avenue's Latin Playboy and Tu y Yo, Ricky's Sky Room in Alhambra—as a grave reminder of a past now passing out of reach.

Burnett says admiringly, "I think Los Lobos have written some of the best social commentary in music of the last half century. They carried on a very courageous tradition, extraordinarily gracefully . . . By their very existence, they *were* a social comment, and they lived up to that. They filled the shoes that they had to fill. The fact of a Chicano punk band at that time, in the late '70s and early '80s, with everything that was going on—there were things that were happening for the first time, and they were certainly one of those things."

Ending without resolution with the psalm-like "Tears of God," *By the Light of the Moon*, for all its propulsive and often joyous music, gazed up at a bad moon rising over a universe of grief, loss, and sometimes incomprehensible pain. It was mature stuff, certainly not always easy to listen to, but undeniably great. The critical community once again responded with favor: The album placed No. 6 among the year's best albums in the *Village Voice*'s 1987 Pazz & Jop Poll, trailing Prince and Bruce Springsteen (again) as well as the Replacements, U2, and John Hiatt. However, with no single to push it, the record duplicated the chart performance of *How Will the Wolf Survive?* finally peaking at No. 47 while selling a respectable four hundred thousand copies.

~~~~~~~~~~~~~~~~~~~~~~~~~~~

Some of the gloom that hung over *By the Light of the Moon* may have been the by-product not just of its songs' themes, but also of the protracted and distressed work that went into the album's making. The band had spent the better part of 1986 in the studio hammering out the record while touring intermittently around the sessions. It was an uncertain time.

A decade after the album's release, Conrad Lozano told me, "At that point, I think we were somewhat overwhelmed by the whole process of the studio, and the formula, and having to work out songs, going to rehearsal, and doing all that. We were pretty much trying to be recording artists by the manual. 'This is how you do it. OK, fine, here we go.' So it took a while for us to put that record together."

Some problems arose. While Louie Pérez was perfectly adequate for Los Lobos' onstage drumming needs, he did not possess the rock-steady timekeeping skills required in the recording studio setting. His tendency to speed up as he played was readily apparent even to nonmusicians at live dates. Ultimately, three other drummers were credited on the album with Louie: Elvis Presley's longtime drummer Ronnie Tutt, Anton Fier of New York's Golden Palominos, and Mickey Curry of Bryan Adams's band.

"There were all these issues about who the drummer was gonna be," Burnett says. "The thing is, when takes [of songs] speed up, you can't [edit] between them, so you have to get a take all the way through. It became a big issue—not for me.

I didn't cause this problem. There were people in the band who wanted a steadier drummer. It fell upon me to try and negotiate through that."

According to Lozano, some resentment built because Burnett was splitting his time between L.A. and his home state while the sessions were in progress: "He was being paid a whole lot of money, plus all the expenses he would incur, going back to Texas every fucking week and flying in and flying back, nice hotels and all that. We thought, man, this guy is really raking it in, isn't he? We thought that was kinda uncool."

The band members claim that Burnett wasn't around when the time came to complete the project.

"At the end of it," Hidalgo says, "trying to get it finished, it started to get a little stretched out. I'd go into the studio by myself to do things to finish it up. Everybody else had already finished their parts. It started to get old. 'Why aren't you guys in the studio, too? Why are you at home having dinner with your families, and I'm over here doing this?' . . . The relationship with T Bone was starting to get a little strained. By the end of that album, he had moved on. Before we were finished with it, he had moved on, so we had to finish it with [engineer] Larry Hirsch. He would pop in, but he was already on to the next thing."

Rosas makes a similar allegation: "There was a period where we lost T Bone Burnett. He had his own personal issues that he was dealing with, and he decided to leave the project. What ended up happening was, me and Larry Hirsch went in there and finished [the album] up . . . I said, 'Fuck it, man, I'm going in to do whatever I can.'"

In a tone of delicate diplomacy, Burnett denies that he walked off the project: "I don't remember that, but that could be. I'm sure I mixed the record, I'm sure I mastered the record. But I leave people alone when they need to be left alone, too. I don't think that's a bad thing. If there's any bad blood from them, it's not returned from me, I'll tell you that."

The most dramatic schism had developed long before the completion of *By the Light of the Moon*, as T Bone Burnett and

Steve Berlin found themselves at nearly constant loggerheads almost from the beginning of the recording sessions.

"By that time," Berlin says, "he and I were disagreeing about a lot of stuff. We had tried to get it worked out. I had a team and he had a team. He had an engineer and I had an engineer, and we had both started working separately from one another. I know that I didn't love what he was doing and he didn't love what I was doing. It was just kind of a weird scene. And, T Bone being T Bone, he then thought that I was the problem. So he tried to get me fired from the band.

"To their credit, they didn't fire me. But as my punishment, such as it was, I had to work on this shitty little bullshit movie that some crazy-ass friend of ours was slapping together. It wasn't going to go anywhere, it wasn't going to do anything. It didn't have any big stars in it.

"It was called *La Bamba*."

– 10 –

NUMERO UNO
WITH A BULLET

La Bamba

In 1987, audiences were not clamoring for a film about the late rock 'n' roll singer–guitarist Ritchie Valens, and not many observers could have augured any great reception for such a picture. As the Hollywood trade magazine *Variety* noted at the time, "There haven't been too many people who died at age 17 who have warranted the biopic treatment."

At that time, Valens had been dead for twenty-eight years, a victim of the small plane crash that also took the lives of his tour mates Buddy Holly and J. P. "Big Bopper" Richardson outside Mason City, Iowa, on February 3, 1959. A product of the city of San Fernando in the San Fernando Valley—"the other side of the hill," in the parlance of L.A. locals—and a former student at Pacoima Junior High, Valens (born Richard Steven Valenzuela) had cut his first session for the fledgling Hollywood label Del-Fi Records in July 1958. Del-Fi's owner, Bob Keane—whose earlier label, Keen, had issued Sam Cooke's first hit, "You Send Me"— had plucked Valenzuela from a group called the Silhouettes and given him a new stage moniker to obscure his Latino roots.

Keane released just two singles by Valens before the musician's untimely death, but both of them reached the charts. The Little Richard–styled rocker "Come On, Let's Go" rose to No. 42 on *Billboard*'s Hot 100 chart. The other 45 was a double-sided winner: the ballad "Donna" peaked at No. 2, while its flip side, "La Bamba"—an adaptation of a Mexican folk dance tune, which the singer had heard as a child—charted separately, topping out at No. 23. A posthumous album comprising the majority of Valens's studio work reached No. 23 in the spring of 1959.

In pop terms, Ritchie Valens was a blip on the national screen: his professional career lasted all of six months, and never yielded a No. 1 record. Yet his status as the first Mexican American rock 'n' roll star kept him cemented in the public consciousness; in Los Angeles, where his career had lifted off thanks to strong local radio support, he enjoyed a long afterlife on such local oldies stations as KRLA, where "Donna" and "La Bamba" were in perennial rotation. The U.S. public at large knew Valens best as a rock legend incarnate, via singer–songwriter Don McLean's immense 1971 hit "American Pie," which had memorably coined the phrase "the day the music died" to denote the day the plane carrying Holly, Richardson, and Valens went down. No mere musician, the Chicano musician was part of American myth.

Nonetheless, the idea of a film about Ritchie Valens saw a long gestation. In a 2011 interview with the Latino cultural website Latinopia, actor–musician Daniel Valdez—who had shared a stage with Los Lobos in 1974—said he first discussed the idea of a biographical film in the early '70s with Taylor Hackford, a young documentary filmmaker who served as Valdez's manager for a time. They pitched the movie to Valdez's label, A&M Records, which was then beginning to move into film production. "Of course, they turned it down," he said.

In the late '70s, Valdez and his brother Luis, Cesar Chavez's former aide and the founding writer–director of the highly politicized Latino troupe El Teatro Campesino, rose to fame with *Zoot Suit*. Originally produced as part of the "New Theatre for Now" series at L.A.'s Mark Taper Forum, the musical drama was a fictionalized recounting of the Sleepy Lagoon murder trial and the subsequent Zoot Suit Riots of 1942–1943. Written and directed by Luis Valdez and starring his younger brother as one of the Sleepy Lagoon defendants, the play became a huge hit in L.A. and its subsequent Broadway production. In 1981, Universal Pictures released a film version of *Zoot Suit*; Daniel Valdez reprised his stage role as Sleepy Lagoon defendant Henry Reyna, as did Edward James Olmos, as "El Pachuco," the highly stylized, zoot-suited character (originated by Daniel Valdez in the show's laboratory production) that served as Reyna's hectoring onstage conscience and the play's Greek, or Chicano, chorus. (Olmos would gain further fame in 1988 portraying Garfield High School math teacher Jaime Escalante in Ramón Menéndez's feature *Stand and Deliver*.) For the film, Luis Valdez chose to cleave closely to the work's theatrical roots, framing the action as a theatrical performance at Hollywood's Aquarius Theatre, where it had in fact enjoyed a popular latter-day run.

Following the success of *Zoot Suit*, Daniel Valdez spent the next five years researching the life of Ritchie Valens. A tip from a friend brought him into contact with Valens's older half brother Bob Morales and younger sibling Mario Valenzuela, and the idea of a Valens film kicked into high gear. Valdez brought the idea back to Taylor Hackford, now a major player in Hollywood as the director of the box office hits *An Officer and a Gentleman* (1982) and *Against All Odds* (1984). Hackford agreed to produce the feature under his New Visions Pictures banner, with Columbia Pictures acting as distributor. Luis Valdez was hired to write the screenplay; ironically, Hackford's directorial services were prohibitively expensive, and he became involved as director of his own rock movie, the Chuck Berry documentary *Hail! Hail! Rock 'n' Roll*, so Valdez ultimately took the directorial reins as well.

Latino rock icon Carlos Santana was hired to co-write the film's score. Clearly, Valens's old hits, roughly produced in mono in 1958, would have to be recut by contemporary musicians to meet the standards of '80s movie sound. As Hackford noted in a promotional featurette about the making of the film, to be called *La Bamba*, "There was only one choice in this film, to me, for recreating Ritchie Valens's music, and that was Los Lobos."

Los Lobos were essentially on a short list of one to remake Valens's material for the feature. They had already recorded "Come On, Let's Go" for their Slash EP, and Valens's "That's My Little Suzie" was a fixture of their live sets. David Hidalgo's sweet tenor was a virtual ringer for Valens's, though in 1986 he was fourteen years older than the late teen star. Both Hidalgo and Cesar Rosas had the chops to replicate Valens's elemental guitar work.

There were other affinities as well. Like Valens, most of the Lobos grew up in Mexican American households where English, not Spanish, was the principal spoken language. And it could be said that by adapting the old Veracruz *son* "La Bamba" to a rock 'n' roll format, Ritchie Valens—the first Latino folk–rocker—had lit the way for Los Lobos' cross-genre work a couple of decades later.

Of course, Los Lobos' paths had crossed those of the Valdez brothers during the group's '70s folk era. From the start, the band enjoyed the endorsement of the Valenzuela family, who had come to admire them after attending a show in Santa Cruz, not far from their home in Watsonville. The members subsequently paid a visit to matriarch Connie Valenzuela and her children, who welcomed them into the family circle.

Pérez told me later, "We sat in their living room as they were bringing out records, photographs, and things that belonged to Ritchie. We were amazed. Then his sister came out of the bedroom holding a soda pop in one hand and a clothes hanger with one of Ritchie Valens's stage outfits in the other and [told] Cesar, 'Why don't you try it on?' Cesar just stood their trembling, his knees knocking."

As much as Los Lobos welcomed the movie opportunity, taking on additional work in the midst of making their second full-length album presented a challenge.

Rosas remembers, "We had probably just started [recording *By the Light of the Moon*], done maybe a couple of weeks of work or something like that, and that's when we got hit up to do the *La Bamba* project. So we had a meeting with Taylor Hackford and Luis Valdez right there in the studio. We were excited that they had asked us. But then we were going, 'OK, we're in the studio on this project, what are we going to do?'"

And so the band doubled down. Work on the soundtrack for *La Bamba* took place in late 1986 at Sunset Sound, the same Hollywood studio that was simultaneously housing the oft-agonizing sessions for *By the Light of the Moon*. Luis Valdez's screenplay called for versions of half a dozen songs, some of which would appear in multiple renderings—Valens's "Come On, Let's Go" (to be recorded a second time by Los Lobos for the soundtrack), "Ooh! My Head," "Donna," and "La Bamba," plus his covers of "Framed" and "We Belong Together."

Working in semi-exile just yards from where the rest of the band continued to labor on *By the Light of the Moon*, Steve Berlin focused his attention on cutting the soundtrack material for the film's demanding director.

"A lot of my job with *La Bamba* was just trying to keep Luis Valdez happy," Berlin says. "He'd come in every day or so, or sometimes two or three times a day. The entire notion of a whole song would change. This went on for weeks, literally weeks . . . I'm sure there are at least four or five different variations for each song."

For the rest of the band, the movie project turned into a virtual sprint.

"We were [recording *By the Light of the Moon*] in the back studio [at Sunset Sound]," Pérez remembers. "Then there's a courtyard with a basketball court, and *La Bamba* was going on in the front studio . . . We would literally run back and forth between the two studios. We'd be doing something for *By the Light of the Moon*, and then someone would run in—'Hey, you guys have got to listen to this'—and then we'd run over there.

"There was another studio to the left, and Prince was [recording] in that one. One time we had to run across the courtyard to listen to something, and in the interim Prince went out there, and he was shooting baskets. We made the turn around the corner, and Prince looked at us, and I think he thought he was going to die. Here are these four Mexicans running . . . toward him. His life probably flashed in front of him."

La Bamba was set for release on July 24, 1987. Warner Bros. scheduled a soundtrack album for June 30; it was to contain the songs cut by Los Lobos, plus tracks from three other musicians seen in the film—the Stray Cats' Brian Setzer (performing "Summertime Blues" as Eddie Cochran), Howard Huntsberry (singing "Lonely Teardrops" as Jackie Wilson), and Marshall Crenshaw (interpreting "Crying, Waiting, Hoping" as Buddy Holly). A new Willie Dixon–produced version of "Who Do You Love" by Bo Diddley, with the Lobos serving as the '50s guitar slinger's backup band, was also included, as were a pair of Lobos covers of non-Valens material—the Sevilles' "Charlena" and Jesse Belvin's "Goodnight My Love"—which played in the background during other scenes.

At the behest of Warner Bros., Los Lobos wound up doing some unanticipated last-minute work tied to the movie, even though the band had heavy touring commitments in Europe and the United States tied to the ongoing promotion of *By the Light of the Moon*.

"We went on the road," Rosas remembers, "and then we got a call from Lenny Waronker. He said, 'Hey, you guys, I know you're tired, I know you're on the road, I know you guys have already done all this work on *La Bamba*, but how would you like to go in there and do a single? Just go in there and play 'La Bamba,' play your ass off, play it the way you guys want to, the way you feel it.' And we said OK. We went in there and recorded it in about three, four hours."

To oversee the recording of the single, the label turned to a musician who had already contributed some keyboard work to *By the Light of the Moon*—a gifted instrumentalist with a budding career as a hit-making producer named Mitchell Froom.

Known primarily as a keyboardist and with one solo album, 1984's *The Key of Cool*, to his credit, Froom had produced albums by L.A. locals Peter Case and Stan Ridgway, among others. But it was his work on the Australian band Crowded House's self-titled 1986 debut that had made him a player commercially: the album, creatively engineered by Tchad Blake, had yielded a pair of Top 10 singles, "Don't Dream It's Over" (No. 2) and "Something So Strong" (No. 7), which together spent a total of forty-five weeks on the national chart.

Froom says of the quickly executed "La Bamba" session, "It was kind of casual. It wasn't, 'This is a real big deal.' I think it was just a shot in the dark. It was [a] one-day [date]. David had a cold that day, and he was saying, 'Should I sing this?' It was that kind of thing. We cut the track in a day, and they went on tour."

The single—which differed from the soundtrack version in its addition of David Hidalgo's accordion, an instrument not heard on either Valens's original or in the film—clocked in very short, at around two minutes and twenty seconds, scarcely longer than the 1958 single. Froom says he suggested extending the track with a coda on which the band played traditional instruments. This was hardly a stretch for them, for they had played "La Bamba" acoustically in the film, in their first big-screen appearance. Los Lobos appear (augmented by musician and ethnomusicologist Fermin Herrera on Veracruz harp) during a sequence in which the virginal Ritchie is taken to a Tijuana brothel by his worldly half brother Bob. In a throwback to their old days as an East Side folk band, they are clad in *guayaberas*, and perform the song *son jarocho* style on *requinto, jarana, bajo sexto*, and *guitarron*. They looked very much the same as they did when they played the "La Bamba" rhythm to close the 1975 *La Cultura* broadcast.

The Slash/Warner Bros. single of "La Bamba" was released in June, a week or two before the album and nearly a month before the nationwide opening of the film. The 45 bowed at No. 84 on the *Billboard* Hot 100 dated June 27; two weeks later it had crept up to No. 60.

On their part, Los Lobos harbored no illusions about any great commercial returns for their soundtrack work, or for the film itself. Lozano says, "We just figured it was going to be a little cold kinda deal, you know. [We thought,] 'Hey, at least it got put out and more people know about Ritchie Valens'—that's how we felt about it. Because, you know, nothing ever came out that good where a Mexican producer or director would be involved."

The band was in Baden-Baden, Germany, in late June when they finally saw a finished cut of *La Bamba*. Says Lozano, "The movie company decided to send us a cut of the film: 'OK, we want you guys to see the film and see what you think before we release the thing.' So they sent the movie over, they bought out a theater for the afternoon, so that we could watch the movie in solitude, just the band. And we watched the film"—and he pauses to laugh at the recollection—"and it fucked us up. It killed us. It was beautiful. I couldn't believe it."

La Bamba received its Hollywood premiere on July 17 at the historic Grauman's Chinese Theatre, directly across the street from the location of the small studio where *Just Another Band from East L.A.* had been mixed in one night in 1977. After the rapturously received screening, some in the audience attended a party and concert at the Palace a few blocks to the east on Vine Street, where performances by Los Lobos and the film's other musical stars were taped for a special on MTV, then the premier television outlet for new music in the United States. VJ Mark Goodman and DJ Wolfman Jack hosted the show, which aired the following week in conjunction with the movie's nationwide opening. (MTV also gave heavy airplay to a video for "La Bamba," directed by Sherman Halsey, which intercut footage from the film with scenes of Los Lobos, abetted by actor Lou Diamond Phillips [who portrayed Valens in the film], playing the song at a carnival erected on the grounds of the Los Angeles Sports Arena.)

And, as *The Buddy Holly Story* had been nine years earlier, *La Bamba* became a sleeper—a surprise smash hit.

Something about Valdez's musical drama pleased reviewers and struck a deep chord in audiences, and the film swiftly became the summer's breakout performer. Perhaps it owed its success to the filmmakers' respectful treatment of Valens's life and career: except for a completely fabricated opening sequence in which the Valenzuelas are working as farm laborers—old UFW hand Valdez clearly could not resist a polemical opportunity—and a highly romanticized depiction of the relationship between Valens and his classmate Donna Ludwig, the script cleaved fairly closely to the facts. (Both Connie Valenzuela and Bob Morales were on the set during filming, which may have encouraged the filmmakers to keep their eyes on the factual ball.)

The picture benefited from engaging performances by its young, largely unknown leads—Filipino American newcomer Lou Diamond Phillips as the sweet yet fiercely ambitious Ritchie, scene-stealing young Latino actor Esai Morales as bad-boy jailbird Bob, Elizabeth Peña as Bob's long-suffering mate Rosie, and fresh-faced Danielle von Zerneck as Donna. (No one seemed to mind that the lupine, wiry Phillips bore scant physical resemblance to the chunky, broad-shouldered Valens.) For most critics and viewers, the warmth and directness of the storytelling and the film's scrupulous attention to period detail made up for the screenplay's often strained dialogue ("I'm gonna be a star, and stars don't fall out of the sky, do they?") Perhaps most importantly, the music was executed with the sort of vitality and authenticity seldom encountered in standard-issue rock biopics.

In its opening weekend, *La Bamba* grossed more than $5.6 million—the majority of its modest $6.5 million budget. The picture benefited from a niche marketing effort by Columbia to target Latino audiences: the English-language film was simultaneously released on a few screens in Spanish-dubbed and Spanish-subtitled versions, and $400,000 of the initial take derived from those houses, according to the *Los Angeles Times*. By the end of its theatrical run, it had grossed $54.2 million, or nearly ten times its budget—a mammoth hit by any standard. It became the No. 15 top-grossing picture of 1987—and it dragged its attendant single and its soundtrack album to glory behind it.

On the eve of *La Bamba*'s release, the titular single entered *Billboard*'s Top 40, at No. 36. Each week of box office success thrust "La Bamba" higher on the chart. For Los Lobos, who were on the road an ocean away, promoting another album that was already dead in the water, the trajectory of the single was nothing less than extraordinary.

Berlin remembers, "The whole time it was like, 'This is nice, but we've got this other record.' And nobody wanted to hear anything about *By the Light of the Moon* . . . We did not think anything was going to happen with 'La Bamba.' We had no inkling it was going to be a big hit. And we were in Europe for most of the thing. We were on a really long European tour. And—pre–cell phone—we would hear, 'Yeah, the record's doing really well on the charts.' 'Yeah, the record's Top 100.' 'Hey, the record's Top 50.' 'Hey, the record's Top 20.' 'Hey, the record's Top 10.' 'Hey, the record's No. 1.' And we couldn't even fucking believe it. 'You've got to be kidding. *That* record?' It was amazing to us."

"La Bamba" reached No. 1 on *Billboard*'s Hot 100 in its tenth week on the chart, in the August 29, 1987, issue of the trade magazine, displacing Madonna's "Who's That Girl." It held the top slot for three weeks; it was knocked from its perch by Michael Jackson's "I Just Can't Stop Loving You," the first single from *Bad*, Jackson's highly anticipated sequel to *Thriller*. Los Lobos—whose only previous chart single, "Will the Wolf Survive?" had topped out at No. 78 during its five-week stay two years earlier—enjoyed a twenty-one-week run with their hit. It was the first single sung entirely in Spanish to reach No. 1 in the United States. The 45 also charted in sixteen other countries, and reached No. 1 in the U.K., France, Spain, and Canada. A second 45 from the soundtrack, the new version of "Come On, Let's Go," rose to No. 21 later in the year and spent fourteen weeks on the chart.

The *La Bamba* album soared as the single reigned, and captured No. 1 for two weeks in September; late that month, the Recording Industry Association of America—the American record industry's trade association and then its primary tracker of sales—certified the record double platinum for shipments of two million copies.

Los Lobos had hit it big. By the end of 1987, they had moved from playing theaters and clubs to opening for the superstar Irish act U2 in some of the biggest stadiums in North America. L.A. punk rock favorites just four years earlier, they were now an international household name.

The question was, what next?

– 11 –

ROOTED AND ROCKED

La Pistola y El Corazón and *The Neighborhood*

The members of Los Lobos understood that the immense success of "La Bamba" and the soundtrack album came with some built-in hazards. Foremost, it was not a success they could really call their own: they had sold two million albums on the back of a long-dead rock 'n' roll star. On the other hand, their own recording *By the Light of the Moon,* made with no small amount of effort and a substantial degree of hurt, had sold no better than the one that preceded it. They ran a significant risk of being a one-hit wonder—a band that had scored what amounted to a novelty hit, with a base of new fans that could desert them as swiftly as they had embraced them.

There was, of course, the time-tested music business option of doing exactly the same thing that they'd already done. They could return to the Valens well again if they chose to. But as Berlin notes, "People were saying, 'Well, when are you gonna do *La Bamba 2?*' There really wasn't anyplace to go with *La Bamba 2,* not that we'd ever think about doing it anyway."

"It spun our heads around, obviously," says Pérez, "because it was a huge thing. But we knew that wasn't us, so I think we had a bit of an identity crisis. I mean, we knew who we were, but we had to get back on track again, and we *knew* we had to get back on track again . . . It's hard to say this without sounding negative, but we had to kind of distance ourselves a little bit from [*La Bamba*]."

Rosas adds, "There was a lot of pressure. It was, 'Wow! What do we do now?' So we decided that if we put out another Los Lobos rock 'n' roll record, it would be a lot of competition with *La Bamba*. People were not gonna understand it. So we said, 'Hey, why don't we just do something completely different?'"

In the end, Los Lobos determined that the best step they could take would be backward—a return to their roots, with a vengeance.

"It's very rare for [Louie Pérez] to say, 'Here's what we need to do,'" Berlin recalls. "And I remember him saying, 'Here's what we need to do. We need to do this record of folkloric stuff, because the world will pay attention because of where we are now, and it'll be good for us.'"

"It was a matter of us doing that thing we did all along," Pérez says. "For us, the way to do it was to go all the way back to the way the band started . . . To take that incredible focus that was on the band because of *La Bamba* and put something out like this, we had a responsibility to take that spotlight and redirect it to something that really meant something to us as a band and to us as a culture."

It's very possible that at that point in the history of the American music industry, Warner Bros. Records was the only label that would have entertained the idea of releasing an album of Mexican folk music sung in Spanish by a multiplatinum rock band. At this critical moment in Los Lobos' history, the company's musical culture and the aesthetic sensibility of its head of A&R, Lenny Waronker, served the interests of the band in a nearly incalculable way. A closer look at the Warner executive's professional history and the way he viewed his job is in order here.

Waronker (pronounced "War-no-cur"), who had overseen the talent end of Warner's business since 1971, was a child of the music industry. His father was Simon "Si" Waronker, a classically trained violinist who had founded the Hollywood pop label Liberty Records in 1955. Si had previously worked as the orchestra contractor at 20th Century Fox, and Liberty's first two singles were drawn from the pens of two brothers he knew from the studio, composers Alfred and Lionel Newman.

Lenny joined the family business as a teenager, working for producer Snuff Garrett at Liberty while studying at UCLA. He managed to place some songs at the label for his friend Randy Newman, a budding writer and the nephew of Alfred and Lionel. In 1966 he joined Warner Bros., where he was mentored by the label's chief executive, Mo Ostin. In the label's A&R department, he recruited producers Russ Titelman and Ted Templeman, who would helm a string of hits for the company; signed left-of-center acts like Newman and Van Dyke Parks, erstwhile collaborator with Brian Wilson of the Beach Boys; and distinguished himself as a producer in his own right, working with such performers as Harpers Bizarre, the Beau Brummels, the Everly Brothers, Gordon Lightfoot, Ry Cooder, Arlo Guthrie, the Doobie Brothers, and James Taylor.

Through the '70s and '80s, Waronker presided over a talent department whose roster included Joni Mitchell, Neil Young, Van Morrison, Rod Stewart, Maria Muldaur, Little Feat, Rickie Lee Jones, and Los Lobos' erstwhile nemesis Paul Simon, to name just a few of the acts who enjoyed long and profitable careers at Warner Bros. The label developed a reputation as the most artist-friendly and risk-taking of the majors, in no small part thanks to Waronker's taste and expertise.

A fondness for the unusual ran in the family, Waronker explained in an obituary for Si Waronker published in the *Los Angeles Times* in 2005: "My father was always one to look at things that were different than the norm. That was what he always said to me—go left."

Pérez says that the band basically bushwhacked Waronker with their plan for the album.

"When Dave and I went to see Lenny about the next record, we brought with us a cassette of us as the acoustic band, from the '70s. We went in and we sat with Lenny and said, 'Hey, listen to this.' And he said, 'Wow!' Nobody really knew that we did that regional Mexican music. He listened to it and he said, 'This is amazing stuff.' He looked at us and we said, 'Yeah, we want this to be our next record.' And he looked at us like, 'Aw, you guys set me up!' And I think we did.

"He said, 'This is something you really want to do?' We said, 'Yeah.' He said, 'OK, make your record. Let me deal with the rest.' 'Dealing with the rest' meant that he'd have to go over to Mo [Ostin] and his people and convince them that it's OK for these guys to commit commercial suicide."

It was a quixotic idea, to be sure, but with the label's biggest single of 1987 and a smash album to their credit, Los Lobos had the leverage to get the go-ahead for their project. Armed with a small budget, and producing themselves with Larry Hirsch engineering, the band dusted off their *requinto, jarana,* and *guitarron* and convened at Sunset Sound, the facility where they had recorded their last two albums, for their folk sessions. It proved to be the fastest work they had done since their original folk album: the record, which they titled *La Pistola y El Corazón,* was recorded and mixed in just five days, on June 13–17, 1988.

"We had a blast," Berlin remembers. "We had so much fun doing it. Every day, it was jokes, and laughing. There was no pressure. It was, 'Let's just do this and put it out.'"

Seven of the album's nine songs—in *son jarocho, huapango, son huasteco, jarabe,* and *ranchera* styles, all of Mexican origin—were either in the public domain or written in the traditional form by modern folk composers. One tune, the Veracruz number "El Canelo," was first recorded on *Just Another Band from East L.A.,* and was part of the repertoire during the era when Frank González was in the band. Five of the tracks were unadorned performances by the core quartet of Rosas, Hidalgo, Pérez, and Lozano; Berlin contributed soprano saxophone on just three numbers. Dollops of percussion were contributed by Berlin, the band's roadie Mouse de la Luz, and Marty Jourard of the Motels.

It is music of the purest simplicity. While the recordings on *La Pistola y El Corazón* may lack the youthful, sometimes sloppy vitality of the performances on *Just Another Band,* there's a grave beauty in the band's determined performances. They also strive to extend the antique forms with some original compositions: Rosas contributes the tequila-soaked *bolero* "Estoy Sentado Aqui," while Hidalgo and Pérez bring the title track, a moonlit ballad of their own with a striking *huapango* guitar introduction by Rosas and a rare lead vocal in Spanish by Hidalgo. Rosas—Los Lobos' original vocalist following Frank González's departure in their folk days—is the lead singer on six of the nine tracks, and performs with soul.

To the millions who had bought the *La Bamba* album, *La Pistola y El Corazón* must have come as a befuddling shock. Without a doubt, virtually no one who knew Los Lobos solely in their hit-making incarnation knew anything about their independently recorded folk debut of a decade before, which was by now such a rarity that even many devoted Lobos fans had never heard it. Almost anyone who had identified the band playing their traditional instruments on-screen in *La Bamba* probably assumed they were miming.

The album was a vexing event for most, and its commercial reception reflected the audience's bewilderment: *La Pistola* peaked at No. 179 on *Billboard*'s album chart, spending just four weeks on the list.

However, the album had never been intended as a commercial entry—it had been calculated as a restatement of artistic and cultural self-definition. In that regard, *La Pistola y El Corazón* proved a brilliant success. At the Shrine Auditorium in L.A. on February 21, 1990, Los Lobos received their second Grammy Award for Best Mexican American Recording for the release. (The award was a much-needed acknowledgment of authenticity in the year that Milli Vanilli was named Best New Artist at the same ceremony; the duo's award would be rescinded that November after it was discovered that they had been miming the work of studio vocalists.)

~~~~~~

Unfortunately, kudos do not pay the mortgage, and in the wake of their second Grammy win Los Lobos had to contemplate the making of a new electric record. The band wanted to produce it themselves, but this time they encountered some pushback from the executives at Warner Bros.

"The label was second-guessing us to death," Pérez recalls.

"It [went] back and forth. A lot of shit was going on, and it took a really long time. It was a real difficult time."

Steve Berlin, who already knew a thing or two about making a particularly grueling Los Lobos record, remembers this period as especially taxing and enervating.

"Here we are," he says, "it's time to make a rock record, and we had developed this relationship with Larry Hirsch, who had engineered half our catalog and engineered *Pistola*. He had never produced anything before. We said, 'Larry's gonna produce it, and we'll just make another rock record.' So we wrote about half of the record, and we brought Larry into rehearsal, and all of a sudden we're seeing a totally different side of Larry . . . That record took, I think, nine months to make, for no good reason other than Larry was having some issues. Larry thought he would never work again unless the record was a smash hit.

"He'd go on the road with us, playing tambourine on all the songs. It was kinda driving everyone crazy, but we went along with it, because we didn't really have a plan B . . . We weren't really listening to our inner voices. We knew that there was something wrong, but we liked Larry, and the stuff sounded good, but his agenda was really, really tough for us. We learned the songs, we'd be ready to record 'em, and then we'd go on the road for three months and play 'em every night and change the parts and get fucking sick of 'em. I literally never wanted to hear them again. And I think everybody in the band felt the same way. We said, 'Wow, this is really fucked up.'"

"It took a long time," Lozano says of the seemingly endless sessions. "For me, as a bass player, I go and do my part and then I'm done, man. [I said to myself,] 'God, why do I even have to go over there today? Well, what if they want me to do something else, or sing a part? I gotta be there.' It was rough."

Many hands contributed to the record. Pérez's drumming was plainly still viewed as a problem, for Jim Keltner and Jerry Marotta, two of the top studio musicians of the day, appear on most of the tracks; Alex Acuña, another pricey pro, is credited with percussion. John Hiatt, then riding high behind some widely praised albums for A&M Records, sang on a couple of tracks, while Levon Helm of the Band dueted with David Hidalgo on "Little John of God." Berlin remembers some sessions with Booker T. Jones and Duck Dunn of Booker T. & the MG's, but they are not credited on the finished album.

"It was like, well, this is what Larry says we need to do, so I guess this is what we're going to do," Berlin says.

The laborious process of making the album that was released on September 4, 1990, as *The Neighborhood* is evident in nearly every note on the record. All of Los Lobos' previous work was characterized by a spirited lightness. The new album was busy and lugubrious, and listening to most of its thirteen tracks requires some actual effort. Any spontaneity or life that had ever existed in the songs was effectively wrung out of them over the long haul of recording sessions. The playing on the album for the most part is leaden, and the thick, murky production only weighs the proceedings down further.

The gravest problem with *The Neighborhood* may have been that Los Lobos didn't appear to have much of anything to say. "There's a deep dark hole and it leads to nowhere," ran the lyrics to one of the songs, and the line could stand as a description of the record's content. Save for the title cut—a hard-hitting prayer for the *barrio* written by Hidalgo and Pérez that Pops Staples of the Staple Singers would memorably record on his *Peace to the Neighborhood* in 1992—and the swirling "Angel Dance," there are no compositions that leave a lasting impression. Hidalgo and Pérez's eleven contributions offer only the most fleeting flashes of inspiration, and none rises to the level of the keenly observed material on *How Will the Wolf Survive?* and *By the Light of the Moon*. Rosas steps up with "I Can't Understand," a number co-written with Willie Dixon, which plays like an outtake by Chicago bluesman Otis Rush. In fact, it's that song and Rosas's other features, "I Walk Alone" and "Jenny's Got a Pony," that offer some welcome, hard-rocking directness on this muddled album.

Rosas himself says, "That record, I didn't feel it, man . . . I don't remember us being in the spirit of it all. I have a hard time listening to it myself. It's one of my least favorite records. I think the songs were there, but I think the production part of it was a little weird for me. I think we could have recorded it a little different. Maybe it could have been a different record."

The Neighborhood never got off the ground commercially. It rose no higher than No. 103 on the album chart, and managed to hang around for nine weeks, largely on the basis of post–"La Bamba" goodwill. It was Los Lobos' worst-performing electric album to date.

To compound this defeat, the band's 1990–1991 tour to support the album, which took them through the United States, Canada, Mexico, Latin America, and Japan (twice), was a financial catastrophe.

"Finally the record was made," Pérez remembers, "and we went out on the road with buses and semis and all this other shit. We're trying to do this big rock thing. And we were still in the process of trying to figure out who we were. I guess everybody said, 'We're gonna be rock stars now? OK.' We went out there and we lost a bunch of money. The making of the record, the release of the record, and the cycle, touring and all that, was just real tough."

"We got caught up in the success of *La Bamba*," says Hidalgo. "We got to hire a lighting guy, get a couple of buses, take our own rigs, and all this stuff. We didn't make any money."

"We overspent," Berlin says. "We had way more production than we needed. We had a lighting guy and sound guy, three guitar techs—just a gargantuan operation. We were the same fucking knuckleheads who had started the whole thing, but we had really lost our way at that point, *really, really* lost our way. So we toured for probably another year and a half, playing the songs that we had gotten tired of.

"We came home owing money . . . At that point we were tired, frustrated, broke. There was a lot of hand-wringing going on at that point. We felt like, all right, we went through this whole thing, we're No. 1 and all this other shit, and here we are, four years later, and we have *nothing* to show for it. We have absolutely nothing to show for all this work, all this time, all this effort."

Exhausted, confused, and somewhere between $30,000 and $70,000 in the hole, Los Lobos returned to Los Angeles at an artistic and spiritual crossroads.

In the Day: A Portfolio of Early Photos by Joel Aparicio

A historic gig: Los Lobos play their first show at a Hollywood punk venue, opening for Joe "King" Carrasco and the Crowns, Oct. 29, 1981. From left: Cesar Rosas, Conrad Lozano, Louie Pérez, David Hidalgo.

Dave Alvin of the Blasters (left) and Cesar Rosas talk bajo sexto, *Club 88, West Los Angeles, 1982.*

(From left) David Hidalgo and Louie Pérez back Phil Alvin of the Blasters at a joint gig, McCabe's Guitar Shop in Santa Monica, late 1982.

The expanded lineup with Steve Berlin, the Music Machine in West Los Angeles, 1982. From left: Cesar Rosas, Conrad Lozano, Louie Pérez, Berlin, David Hidalgo.

*David Hidalgo with his arsenal—Telecaster, steel guitar, accordion—
at Rismiller's (formerly the Country Club), Reseda, 1982.*

Cesar Rosas, playing one of his many, many
left-handed axes, Rismiller's, 1983.

Ecstasy: Conrad Lozano, Rismiller's, 1982.

*Doing the hand jive: Recording . . . and a time to dance,
Warner Bros. Studios, North Hollywood, 1983.*

Louie Pérez recording . . . and a time to dance, Warner Bros. Studios, 1983.

*Hometown heroes: Cesar Rosas entertains the crowd,
Lincoln Park, East Los Angeles, 1985.*

*Hitting the big time: Stage view, the Roxy, on
the Sunset Strip, West Hollywood, 1983.*

Working the room: Steve Berlin, St. Mary's, San Antonio, Texas, 1983.

- 12 -

LET'S TRY *THIS*

Kiko, Latin Playboys, and *Colossal Head*

In an attempt to mix things up and shake off the malaise into which the band had sunk, David Hidalgo and Louie Pérez decided to try something different. In doing so, they opened the most intensely exciting chapter of Los Lobos' creative career.

Pérez and Hidalgo established a dedicated space in which to work, almost a creative office. "We actually set up a writing place," Pérez says. "We rented behind a bookstore in Whittier, where we both lived at the time. We said, 'Let's get serious about writing songs for this record.' The paper was all nice and clean and the pencils were all sharpened."

Says Hidalgo, "We'd go down there a couple of times a week. We were back to sitting in a room face to face, banging stuff out, seeing what we could come up with. We'd talk about ideas, and bullshit. So that's how that process that became *Kiko* started—the first half of it, 'Two Janes,' 'Rio de Tenampa,' 'Peace,' all those songs came out of that period."

"I noticed something was changing," Pérez adds. "As we started writing the songs, I thought, 'This is moving somewhere.' I didn't know what was propelling it, what was moving it, but it felt different."

With a few highly impressionistic songs in hand, the band decided to lay them down on tape, with Paul duGré serving as engineer. DuGré had already developed something of a rep on the L.A. punk scene, working with X, Divine Horsemen, Dave Alvin, and Claw Hammer. He had also recorded a 1988 album by Stevie Salas of Tierra, and worked on the soundtrack for the 1991 feature *The Mambo Kings*, the movie adaptation of Oscar Hijuelos's Pulitzer Prize–winning novel *The Mambo Kings Play Songs of Love*, which included Los Lobos' English-language version of the Oscar-nominated song "Beautiful Maria of My Soul." DuGré also served as an engineer on *Great Big Boy*, a 1991 Leo Kottke album produced by Steve Berlin.

The band demoed their new material at duGré's small studio, Paul and Mike's, in downtown L.A. The facility was located "on the Nickel," in the heart of the city's Skid Row, the central vortex for thousands of L.A.'s homeless; the experience of recording there inspired a new Pérez–Hidalgo composition, "Angels with Dirty Faces."

Berlin says, "We started making these demos. All of a sudden it was, 'Wow. That works. That sounds like us. That's a record I'd want to hear again and not want to kill myself if I had to hear it twice.' We started feeling good about ourselves and what we were doing and why we were doing it. We sort of found ourselves again."

Seeking input on their material, the Lobos brought the demos to Lenny Waronker, who had been promoted to the presidency of Warner Bros. Records in 1989. Again displaying the keen instincts that made him one of the most respected executives in the music industry, Waronker suggested that Los Lobos record again with Mitchell Froom and his creative engineer Tchad Blake, who had been brought in to record the one-off track "Angel Dance" on *The Neighborhood*.

Noting that the song was the only number on that album not co-produced by Larry Hirsch and the band, Berlin says that the track had a "totally different vibe, totally different set-up . . . I'm not sure why we did it that way, but that really was in every respect the first *Kiko* song. It was the same [approach]— 'Let's put this crazy *huapango* rhythm on this pop track and see where it goes.' That was pretty much one of the first times we'd ever gone that way, where we'd taken a traditional two-hundred-year-old ethnic rhythm and written a pop song in English."

Beyond the unusual sonic force of "Angel Dance," which

undoubtedly had caught the Warner executive's attention, Waronker was probably acknowledging with his suggestion the huge impact that Froom had made on Los Lobos' career with his production of the "La Bamba" single. Also, at that moment Froom had maintained a solid commercial track record in the business: apart from his work with Crowded House, which had continued on the Aussie group's *Temple of Low Men* and *Woodface*, he had recently produced Paul McCartney's *Flowers in the Dirt* (the ex-Beatle's collaboration with Elvis Costello), Costello's own *Mighty Like a Rose*, and Richard Thompson's much-admired *Rumor and Sigh*.

As it happened, Froom and Blake, who had been working together for three years, had themselves reached something of a pivotal point in their collaborative association.

"We hadn't really found ourselves," Froom says. "We did some things that did pretty well, but it was all [about] trying to be as good as other people, rather than having found our own thing. Lenny suggested, 'Try it out and see what happens.' That's where it started. That was the beginning of it for us as a team."

He adds that he and Blake linked up with Los Lobos at a critical time in the band's career, and under the perfect circumstances for some adventurous music-making.

"I think that [the band] had seen things build up, and then things start to fade away," says Froom. "It had sort of started to lose steam, and had lost vitality, and they were not doing as well. [For them] it was really just, throw caution to the wind and try to please yourself."

Froom credits Waronker's work as a creative facilitator with beginning a new artistic chapter in the band's career: "[Los Lobos] had a very rare thing, which I haven't encountered since, which was a record company president who had a meeting and said, 'How do we move this forward artistically?' I haven't heard those words from a label person since, and that was in 1991. I had never had that conversation before. It's so inspiring. If they'd had a different guy who said, 'We need a big rock hit,' it never would have happened."

When Froom and Los Lobos, who would share production

credit, convened with engineer Blake at Sound Factory West in West Hollywood for the beginning of formal sessions for the new album, the original demos—which had a grimy, off-center feel to them—served as the principal inspiration for the work to follow.

"They're really distorted," Froom says. "We started paying attention to that—'That has a thing about it that we don't want to get all cleaned up. What can we do?'"

In fact, five of the tracks recorded at Paul and Mike's—"Rio de Tenampa," "Peace," "Arizona Skies," "Two Janes," and "Short Side of Nothing"—appear on the finished album, with additional engineering by Blake. A comparison of the demos that were subsequently issued to the finished tracks shows that the band and production team were keying off the dirtiness of the initial recordings. The album's "Peace," a lyrical cousin of "The Neighborhood," bulks up Hidalgo's cycling acoustic guitar riff with stabbing electric guitar lines, hollow percussion, and groans of twisted baritone sax; "Whiskey Train" amplifies the filthy sound of Hidalgo's electric lead, and is punctuated at its climax by the sound of breaking glass, a gunshot, and a woman's scream; and "Rio de Tenampa" is boiled down to its essence, with a couple of original verses in English excised and the accompaniment of the local La Chilapeña brass band compressed and electronically processed into a veering, drunken waltz, performed by what sounds like an enormous, blaring car horn.

The approach to the instrumental "Arizona Skies" exemplifies the kind of go-for-broke studio aesthetic that came into play during the sessions.

Froom recalls, "It was one of the first records where people would hear things that were intentionally distorted. We did it often to make something sound old. I remember the moment it happened. Tchad had brought in this little guitar pedal called the SansAmp, which simulated amplifiers. It had a lot of fine controls on it. We had started working on 'Arizona Skies,' and we'd heard the demo, and the demo sounded better than the [new] recording. The recording sounded very clean, while on the demo the percussion sounded like it was coming from the '40s or something. It had this beautiful dark sound. So [we said], 'The pedal, let's put that on the percussion and see what happens.'

"All of a sudden the whole track sounded like something that none of us had heard before. Today it would be a very common type of sound, but people weren't trying it [then]. The sessions were filled with moments like that—'Oh, we used this pedal to distort the percussion, now what if we use it to put it on the bass drum and see what happens.' It was that kind of free spirit with sound, and also with arrangement at the same time."

The producer himself—billed as "Mitchell Froom and His House of Keyboards" in the album's credits—contributed to the otherworldly density of the recordings. The arcane instruments he employed during the sessions included the Chamberlin, a '50s-vintage keyboard employing prerecorded effects tapes that was a precursor of the Mellotron, and the Optigan, a similar device invented in the late '60s that used optical discs. What sounds like massed, overdubbed horns playing the Duke Ellington–inspired nursery-rhyme theme of "Kiko and the Lavender Moon" is in fact the product of Froom's Chamberlin.

Froom and Blake went to extreme lengths to ensure that something out of the ordinary would manifest itself on tape.

"Tchad would do all kinds of crazy stuff," Pérez recalls. "We were sticking mics down drainpipes and in the middle of a galvanized trash can. Mitchell would bring in the Optigan and all this crazy keyboard stuff, backward guitars—all this stuff that we were really having fun with. But at the same time, something else was happening. Because we had cleaned the slate, we were wide open for things to come. We had cleaned out the cobwebs. We had the Roto-Rooter clean everything out, and everything started coming through. What was at work, I could never put my finger on. I still don't know what that was."

"A huge part of it was the way Tchad interpreted the sound," Berlin says. "I just remember going in and doing something, or David doing something, and we'd come back into the control room, and Tchad had done something so miraculously amazing to the sound, you'd say, 'Oh, my God, I'd never be able to do that again if I tried. I don't know how the fuck I did it!'"

Hidalgo also offers admiring testimony about Blake's free-wheeling studio necromancy: "We didn't know what Tchad was doing. He'd mic it. Then we'd go in and listen to it, and it would be—*pheeewww!*—this other world we had in the control room, the way Tchad heard what we were doing and then interpreted it. Wow! He'd gone on to something bigger and better than where it started.

"We started to enjoy that. We were listening back to 'Angels with Dirty Faces,' and we said, 'Some backward guitar would sound good.' So Tchad whips on the tape and says, 'Go ahead. Try it.' *It's that easy? That's it?* We were having fun in the studio now."

The process of making the album was such a radical departure that it flabbergasted some of the participants. Lozano confesses, "When I started hearing some of the stuff, I thought, 'This is . . . this is *bizarre.*' It felt a little bit like how [the Beach Boys'] Mike Love used to feel about some of Brian Wilson's songs: '*Weird,* man! This isn't *right.*' You know, one of those kinds of feelings? Especially 'Kiko'—'That sounds like "Three Blind Mice!" What the fuck?' But then it started to grow on me—'OK, now I get a better picture of what we're doing here.'"

When the work was completed, the band knew they had created something out of the ordinary.

"The record had its own life," Pérez says. "When it came down to, 'What are we gonna call this record?' I said, 'Well, this is kind of like a living thing. Maybe it doesn't need to be called something. Maybe it needs to be *named* something, just like you name your kid.' This is a person, this record, with all the wrinkles and dimples and everything else."

Hence *Kiko.*

Berlin says, "I've never been part of another record, on any level, that seemed so dreamlike at every turn," and indeed *Kiko* exists in a kind of unconscious space, suffused with the magical realism of Gabriel Garcia Marquéz. A quarter of the album's sixteen songs—"Dream in Blue," "Wake Up Dolores," "Kiko and the Lavender Moon," "Saint Behind the Glass"—actually take place in a dream state. That air of reverie is heightened throughout by the suggestive attack of the music. The literalism of Los Lobos' earlier music—the earthiness of their Mexican folkloric roots, the roadhouse rumble of their rockabilly, blues, and R&B material—has been transmuted into something rich and strange. Tradition-bound instruments—violin, banjo, accordion—are now deployed in an almost entirely nontraditional manner, and even Berlin's horns are used in new, choral ways. The *son jarocho* form of Pérez and Hidalgo's "Saint Behind the Glass," with Veracruz harp work by Fermin Herrera, animates a primal nocturnal vision of religious intensity, with a rare, vulnerable lead vocal by Pérez; Rosas's Bobby Womack–inspired "Wicked Rain" quivers with an underpinning of apocalyptic prophesy. Several numbers glide on hypnotic tape loops and subdued beds of unfettered noise.

Yet, for all the dream-play at work in *Kiko*, the album is simultaneously grounded in the almost reportorial realism found on *How Will the Wolf Survive?* and *By the Light of the Moon*. It contains some of the band's darkest musings about society, on homelessness ("Angels with Dirty Faces"), teen suicide ("Two Janes," inspired by a real-life double suicide Pérez had read about), alcoholism ("Whiskey Train"), and violence both domestic ("Reva's House") and political ("Peace"). But these subjects are surveyed in songs that seem to hover somewhere in the middle of the air.

Kiko arrived in stores on May 26, 1992—less than a month after widespread civil disorder wracked Los Lobos' hometown, following a not-guilty verdict in the criminal trial of four police officers charged in the beating of black motorist Rodney King. The album's closing message—"Peace to the world"—seemed altogether timely.

At its release, it was a remarkable and stunning thing to hear. Nothing on the market sounded vaguely like it. And, on the basis of *The Neighborhood*, even the most prescient listener couldn't have anticipated that Los Lobos would vault into such rarified territory. It was greeted as the band's high-water mark: at year's end, *Kiko* topped the annual *Los Angeles Times* critics poll, beating out *3 Years, 5 Months and 2 Days in the Life of . . .* by Arrested

Development, the hip-hop group that eventually won the 1993 Grammy as Best New Artist. The album also placed No. 6 in the *Village Voice*'s Pazz & Jop Poll. The band's barrier-breaking performance extended to the visual side: director Ondrej Rudavsky's traffic-stopping video for "Kiko and the Lavender Moon," a mind-bending, hallucinogenic melding of George Méliès and Timothy Leary, collected MTV's Breakthrough Video Award in 1993.

The accolades accorded *Kiko* didn't translate into renewed sales for the band: the album peaked at No. 143 on the *Billboard* chart and spent a mere ten weeks there. However, it had incontestably done what it had set out to achieve: it had completely revitalized Los Lobos creatively, in exclamatory fashion. Now, no one could ever simply peg them as "that Chicano band that covered 'La Bamba.'" They had made a record beyond category, and one of the incontestably great albums ever created by an American rock band.

～～～～～～～～～～～～～～～～～～～～～～～～

Music was spilling out of them, and Hidalgo and Pérez, who had written fourteen of the sixteen tracks on *Kiko*, were carried along by the album's momentum. And so a side project was born.

Pérez says that as work on *Kiko* continued, "we were writing, coming up with more shit and more shit. At one point Mitchell said, 'Hey, we gotta stop sometime.' David and I just kept going. We had this four-track TASCAM cassette machine, and we'd do this stuff in the middle of the night, and you had to be real quiet, because you didn't want to wake anybody up. It had something to do with the sound of those basic tracks."

"Usually," Hidalgo adds, "with Louie and I, when an album's finished, we're done. We shut it off. 'OK, it's over. Cool.' We know when we're done—we have no more ideas. But when we finished *Kiko*, the ideas kept coming. I'd go home, and when the kids and the family'd go to bed, I'd set up the little four-track cassette in the kitchen and just put down ideas. What I learned from *Kiko* was just goofing around and having fun and not worrying about it—let's see what happens. That went on, and I had about twelve, fifteen things, and I said, 'I don't know what it is—check it out.' Louie said, 'Ah, this isn't Lobos stuff. This is different.' I think that was the first time we split up the [songwriting] roles—I gave Louie the music, and he wrote lyrics to it.

"I said, 'Do whatever you want to do with what you hear here.' Then he gave them to me, but he didn't tell me what lyrics went to which song. He gave me the lyrics back, and he said, 'OK, *you* do what *you* want. Put 'em where you think they fit.' And most of the time we had the same idea. So we got that together and sent it to Mitchell, and he liked the idea. So we went to Lenny and told him what we wanted to do. He said, 'How much is it gonna cost?' 'Oh, twenty-five grand.' 'Just do it.'"

Pérez continues: "I played it for Mitchell and he said, 'Wow. What do you want to do?' I said, 'I don't know. A record?' He said, 'Yeah! I think it is ... *This* is the record.'"

Froom, who enlisted his studio sidekick Blake to play bass and massage the tapes, recalls, "I said, 'Well, let's just use those—start there and see what we can do.' So we took those and bounced them to twenty-four-track and worked on them a little bit, and two weeks later that record was done ... [I said,] 'We have all this tape, what are we gonna do?' And Tchad said, 'Well, I've got all this ambient stuff, [from] when I was in Africa. Let me put some of that behind it, get rid of some of the hiss.' It was that kind of frame of mind."

The group and its collectively produced album took their name from the Latin Playboy, the derelict nightspot on East L.A.'s Brooklyn Avenue (now Cesar Chavez Avenue), name-checked in Rosas's "Set Me Free (Rosa Lee)"; it stands on the boulevard to this day, its signage faded to illegibility. The experimental bent that characterized *Kiko* was taken to a heightened level. Propelled by Hidalgo's hot-wired guitars and Froom's chameleonic keyboards, the music seemed to draw inspiration from anywhere and everywhere—the Afro-beat of Fela Kuti, Roger Miller's "King of the Road," the gnarled avant-blues of Captain Beefheart and His Magic Band. Random sound bleeds into the mix (deliberately)—a TV in a neighboring room, police sirens screaming in the midnight distance—while some tracks are built around aural debris from Blake's library of "found sound," like "Viva La Raza," with its giggling children yelling out their Chicano pride, or "Mira!" which careens on the noise of a street parade. Almost every loping, percussive track is distorted to a lather, making a jarring bed for Pérez's elusive before-dawn lyrics.

Released in March 1994, the delicious and electrifying *Latin Playboys* didn't so much as scratch the charts, but it gave the band members an opportunity to scratch an artistic itch. Its unusually spontaneous creation set the stage for what was to come.

~~~~~~

Kiko had been built on a surfeit of excitedly created material. The opposite would prove to be true in the case of its successor, which was fabricated virtually out of thin air.

In 1995, Los Lobos spent much of their time at work on the most demanding soundtrack project they had undertaken since *La Bamba*: writing and performing the music for the extravagant action picture *Desperado*, a semi-sequel to *El Mariachi*, the ultra-low-budget 1992 sensation directed by the Texas-born Mexican American director–writer–editor–cinematographer Robert Rodriguez. The great majority of *Desperado* was scored by the Lobos, and some Latin Playboys music was also employed, but it also included several songs by Tito & Tarantula, a band fronted by the group's old L.A. punk colleague Tito Larriva, who also played one of the movie's greasier villains.

Berlin remembers, "*Desperado* became an unbelievably extreme exercise in how much music we could possibly generate, because Robert is just a voracious consumer of music. In a normal film score—almost any film score that isn't a major musical—in ninety minutes of screen time there might be thirty to forty minutes of music, if you took every single cue and added it up. It's between a third and a fifth of the picture, roughly. In Robert's movies, it's almost nonstop music. If the scenes don't have music, he asks for music to shoot to. He does it all himself, and he likes to have rhythm in the headphones while he's shooting a scene. We were willing participants in that game. We gave them so much stuff, *so* much stuff. It was insane."

Their work on *Desperado* would garner Los Lobos their third Grammy Award, as the triptych of themes "Mariachi Suite" was named Best Pop Instrumental Performance of 1995. But the cost was steep. Scheduled sessions for another Lobos studio album were right ahead. As far as new material was concerned, the larder was suddenly bare.

"Literally the day after the Sunday night that we handed [the music for *Desperado*] all in and we were officially done—that Monday morning we're in the studio," Steve says. "And Robert had sucked every single idea that we had between all of us out of us. Every usable nugget we had lying around we gave to Robert, and then we started a record.

"So, OK, now what? Hidalgo goes, 'Well, what would [bluesman] Jimmy Reed do?' He just walked into the studio and made a record, and that's kind of what we did. That record occupies a very warm spot in my heart, just because of the provenance of it."

With essentially no new material at their disposal, Los Lobos were forced to create a record on the fly. The album that became known as *Colossal Head*—its title inspired by the mammoth stone sculptures carved by the Olmec Indians of Mexico's Veracruz region, and possibly playing off the musical term "head arrangement," denoting an off-the-cuff orchestration— essentially sprang forth like Athena from Zeus's brow.

"Some stuff on *Kiko* was invented on the fly, here and there, but there were more ideas up front," says Froom, who returned to co-produce with the band, with Blake now taking a producer credit as well. "*Colossal Head* was much more invented in the studio."

Pérez says, "*Colossal Head* for me always was this riff record. Everything was built on a riff. Dave was listening to a lot of ZZ Top at the time, and a lot of what I was getting from Dave at that point was riff-based tunes."

Berlin adds, "Because we didn't really have time to compose anything, or nobody got anything together before the record started, it's all just very, very simple structurally, and therefore [the songs] kind of play themselves. There's lots of room in the groove and lots of room in the construction."

Abetted by drummer Pete Thomas of Elvis Costello's Attractions (a veteran of the *Kiko* sessions), percussionists Efrain Toro and Victor Bisetti (the latter of whom was now sharing onstage drum chores with Pérez), and keyboardist Yuka Honda of the experimental New York band Cibo Matto, Los Lobos let their freak flag fly during the sessions at Hollywood's Sunset Sound. In every way more extreme and kinetic than the record that preceded it, it has an in-the-moment feel—especially on the album-opening "Revolution," an insistent farewell to the days of Chicano power stoked by Hidalgo's angular guitar work, and on "Mas y Mas," a thunderous rocker with blowout work by Hidalgo and an unfettered vocal in slangy Spanglish:

> *Let's go* bailando, noche*'s lookin' fine*
> *Jump into the* caro, *drink a bunch of wine*
> *Don't tell us nothin', we look outta sight*
> *Tell a lotta lies and go outside and fight*
> Uno pa delante, otro pa detras
> Dame chispas *honey,* dame mas y mas

"'Mas y Mas,' that's pretty much exactly what happened," Froom recalls. "I don't think there's any overdubs, [though] we did the vocal after. There were six, seven people playing, and the solo happened live. It was really a band-in-the-room kind of record, in many ways. 'Revolution' was the same. We just got the noise going."

Hidalgo, who says *Colossal Head* is his favorite among the band's work, points to certain daring precursors as the prime influences on the album's off-the-map approach.

"There's more fun involved in the sound," he says. "And part of that, too, was [a product of] working with Willie Dixon. When we did 'Who Do You Love' for *La Bamba*, Willie produced the session. He organized the band and arranged it on the spot . . .

Also, from the very beginning, Captain Beefheart was a big influence. By that time, I had met him. I had started to talk to him over the phone, and became a friend of Don [Van Vliet, aka Captain Beefheart].

"In my mind, in whatever I did, there were two people—Beefheart, and Bo Diddley. They always did things differently. Even if it was a straight blues, Bo would find a way to make it bolder, somehow. He'd always play it like no one else. Beefheart, if it was a straight-up blues, he found a way to twist it and turn it into something that wasn't standard blues. Those guys, and Willie Dixon, are the ones who helped guide all the references for what became *Colossal Head*."

To be sure, the work of Beefheart—the California desert visionary whose hyper-experimental music and askew lyricism animated the monolithic 1969 opus *Trout Mask Replica* and several subsequent avant-rock classics—cast a huge shadow at this juncture. Hidalgo's sideways playing on "Revolution" genuflects deeply to the work of Beefheart's guitarist Zoot Horn Rollo, while the Pérez–Hidalgo track "Everybody Loves a Train" is essentially an homage to "Click Clack," a number from Beefheart's 1972 release *The Spotlight Kid*.

Hidalgo and Pérez left a deep imprint on the album with such other spry numbers as "Manny's Bones," a shuffling comedic funeral song for an old *vato*, and the title track, a jerking "dance tune" whose lyrics command, "Do the colossal head." But Rosas also made his presence known, contributing "Little Japan," a clattering ballad co-written with Pérez that resembled a Sly & the Family Stone outtake, and "Maricela," a percolating Latin number that introduced the rump-shaking Colombian/Panamanian *cumbia* rhythm to the band's rhythmic arsenal.

"I love that record," Rosas says. "It's like part two of *Kiko*, but more balls-to-the-wall. On *Kiko*, we discovered what we wanted to do, and we already had the green light to do it. [*Colossal Head*] was a bit more of the *Kiko* thing, but . . . [with] crazier songs."

Less intensely focused and mysterious than *Kiko*, but still layered with risky sonic daring, and more loosely jointed and more overtly rocking, *Colossal Head* was released in May 1996. It attracted a larger audience than its predecessor, climbing to No. 81 on the *Billboard* album chart—not a huge hit, by any stretch, but still proof that Los Lobos' left-field music could leave an impression with pop listeners.

- 13 -

SIDE TRACKS

Papa's Dream, Soul Disguise, Houndog, Dose

Latin Playboys was the first Los Lobos side project of note, but the Lobos themselves were billed atop an album that was, in essence, another side project, for it featured no new music of their own.

In 1994, the band was approached to record an album for Music for Little People, a children's music label operated by a Northern California entrepreneur named Leib Ostrow. According to Rosas, sessions for the project—which entailed recording both kid-friendly rock 'n' roll songs (including, of course, "La Bamba") and Mexican folk tunes—were already in progress when a key player was brought into the picture.

"We tracked it over at my home studio in Rowland Heights," Rosas recalls. "We just started tracking songs. What happened was, maybe about three-quarters into the record . . . [Ostrow] asked us if we wanted anybody to narrate it. None of us wanted to take the microphone to narrate it. Right then and there, I said, 'Son of a bitch! Lalo Guerrero!' And everybody went, 'Wow! Yeah, man!'"

Lalo Guerrero, the grand old man of East L.A. music, was a natural to take the starring role in such a project. His association with Los Lobos dated back more than a decade: in 1981, Hidalgo and Lozano had been enlisted to rerecord some of Guerrero's parodies—"I Left My Car in San Francisco," "Tacos for Two," and "Pancho Lopez"—for an album issued by the independent L.A. label Ambiente.

"We'd known him forever," says Louie. "His nightclub, Lalo's, was on Brooklyn Avenue in East L.A. If I'd had a good arm I could hit it with a baseball from my house ... When Lalo came in, it became Lalo's record. The guy was larger than life, and it was fantastic."

The Chicano star—who of course had his own experience in the children's market with his Las Ardillitas records—became the narrator and centerpiece of *Papa's Dream*, which mated the music (curated by Eugene Rodriguez) with a script by Phillip Rodriguez and Al Carlos Hernandez. In keeping with its target audience, the narrative was thin but easy to follow: "Papa Lalo" (Guerrero) takes his "sons" (Los Lobos) and "grandkids" (the Children's Coro of Los Cenzontles Musical Arts Center of San Pablo) on a "Chicano blimp" trip to Mexico for his eightieth birthday *pachanga*. Backed by the band, Guerrero sang the lead on two traditional numbers that dated back to the Lobos' folk days, "Cielito Lindo" and "De Colores." In a switch, Cesar Rosas took the lead on both the rock and folk versions of "La Bamba," while Sam the Sham's "Wooly Bully," the Hollywood Flames' "Buzz, Buzz, Buzz," and Clarence "Bon Ton" Garlow's "Route 90" all received old-school Lobos treatment.

The release of the baldly recorded *Papa's Dream* in early 1995, hard on the heels of the sonically extravagant *Latin Playboys*, was a bizarre juxtaposition. But the set reached its target audience, and ultimately received a Grammy nomination for Best Children's Album. The only pity is that the project didn't lead to deeper work pairing Los Lobos and Guerrero, who died in 2005 at the age of eighty-eight.

~~~~~~~~~~~~~~~~~~~~~~~~~~~~~~~~~~~~~

Enlivened by the highballing experimentation of their '90s work, the Lobos' principal songwriters all embarked on side projects that saw release in 1999. Each affords some heightened insight into the members' musical roots.

Rosas—who recorded his solo debut *Soul Disguise* for the independent label Rykodisc in the garage studio of his Rowland Heights home—takes a low-key view of his own solo work.

"Louie and Dave always wanted to do that thing, that Latin Playboys thing," he says. "Then there was me . . . I was encouraged by some friends of mine, and I said, 'OK, I'll give it a shot.' [There was] no pressure at all. It was just a fun thing to do. I recorded at my house by myself, with a couple of guest musicians here and there. That was pretty much it."

Anyone listening to *Soul Disguise* in a blindfold test would be able to identify the artist before the end of the first chorus on the first track. It's the work of Los Lobos' most ardent traditionalist, and the sound of the album dates as far back in the band's history as "Don't Worry Baby"—or, for that matter, as far back as "Sabor a Mi." The album is roots–rock all the way.

The collection—comprising ten Rosas originals (four of them co-written with ex–Asleep at the Wheel member Leroy Preston) and two covers—was recorded with a posse of like-minded sidemen that included the Lobos' percussion regular Victor Bisetti, keyboardist Eddie Baytos of the zydeco-inflected L.A. band the Nervis Brothers, and accordion star Flaco Jimenez (a fellow member of the all-star Tex–Mex project Los Super Seven, whose 1998 debut also featured David Hidalgo and was produced by Steve Berlin). "Little Heaven" and "Racing the Moon" owe an obvious debt to the inspiration of Dave Alvin's writing for the Blasters; "E. Los Ballad #13" is the sort of romantic, slow-burning R&B that would light up the request line on the Chicano-friendly oldies station KRLA; and the two-step "Angelito" and the *bolero* "Adios Mi Vida" call up memories of Rosas's days as the Lobos' ballad specialist. On the title track, he reminds everyone with some powerful bold-as-love Hendrix-styled solo work that he is not merely holding David Hidalgo's coat in Los Lobos' guitar front line.

Rosas played a two-month club tour supporting *Soul Disguise*, a highly listenable summation of everything he does well, in the spring of 1999. To date the album has not spawned a sequel, though he says he has two solo albums in the can—one a collection of traditional music in Spanish, the other a rock 'n' roll record.

Like much of Cesar's record, *Houndog,* the lone album released by David Hidalgo's eponymous duo unit, is a homemade project that draws deeply from the blues, but it sounds quite unlike any other blues record ever made.

The album, which ultimately found an unlikely home on Columbia Records, was the product of a chance encounter between Hidalgo and Mike Halby, a journeyman guitarist who had worked with the L.A. blues–rock group Canned Heat in the early 1980s.

Hidalgo recalls, "There was a music store in La Habra called Red Duck. It was a guitar shop; Johnny Kallas was the guy who ran the place. I'd take my guitars in there to get repaired. It was kind of like a [neighborhood] barbershop—musicians would go there to get repairs and hang out and bullshit. Johnny was a friend of Mike's—that's how I met him. Johnny was the one who said, 'You know, you can probably come up with something together.'

"We started talking about how much we hated a lot of the modern blues records. They were so light-blues. I was listening to a lot of Jimmy Reed, and Don & Dewey . . . That's what we were shooting for. And that's what came out."

Houndog was recorded in a makeshift studio off the kitchen of Halby's L.A. house. Hidalgo works in the background, supplying guitar, quivering fiddle work in the manner of Don "Sugarcane" Harris of Don & Dewey, and the uncredited drum work. Halby takes the lead vocals, and it is his deep, often agonized groan—its effect heightened by manipulation of the tape speed on some numbers—that is the focal point of the record's nighttime vibe.

"We wanted a kind of underwater sound, and we did that at different degrees, depending on the song," Hidalgo says. "It's a lot like [the Beatles'] 'Strawberry Fields Forever.' The reason John [Lennon] sounds that way on the record is because they slowed the tape down. We thought, 'Hey, he did it. We can do it, too.' We had heard the master of 'Sweet Little Sixteen' by Chuck Berry . . . I thought, I bet they sped it up to make him sound younger and more whitey-friendly. We weren't the first to do it."

Houndog is a spare, narcotized record, a *blues moderne* nocturne that takes Jimmy Reed's basic format and winds it down to an unnerving crawl. It's music that gets under one's skin and stays there, like an itch that can't be scratched. Of the album's nine tracks, the standout is an oozing remake of Junior Parker's "Change My Style," on which Halby's double-tracked call-and-response singing sloshes affectingly against Hidalgo's prickling violin.

An appearance at the South by Southwest Music Festival in 1999 was one of Houndog's few live dates, though David says a second album was completed and never released. Mike Halby died in October 2008.

~~~~~~

The Latin Playboys had been posited as a one-off event employing the overflow of *Kiko*-era compositions, but in 1999 an opportunity arose for a second album by the ad hoc group.

Froom says, "A friend of mine, [A&R vice president] Yves Beauvais at Atlantic, loved the band, and he wanted to sign us, but he said, 'Well, if you guys do a tour, we'll make a record. So I said, 'Sure I will! We'll have enough things to play—we'll have two albums.' So that was the only time we ever toured. It was about six weeks."

Froom describes *Dose*, the sophomore Latin Playboys album, as "a more spirited kind of music. It was more fun to work on, and it all comes out of David sitting around, goofing around, trying to come up with something cool. So you'll get something like 'Mustard.' That's just him sitting at home making this cool riff, and adding percussion with a teacup—I don't even know what he was using. It's more spontaneous and loose."

Even more fabulist at its heart than *Latin Playboys*, *Dose* bore the cover legend "El Disco Es Cultura," and its songs' subject matter ranges through the East Side experience in a way its precursor's songs did not. "Cuca's Blues" recounts the long-ago romantic adventures of a barrio woman who rode to the downtown L.A. clubs on the now-disappeared rails of the "Red Car" trolley. "Paletero" celebrates the neighborhood's shaved-ice vendors and their ubiquitous pushcarts. Best of all, Pérez's spoken-word piece "Ironsides" depicts a reluctant trip to an outdoor movie in the bed of a truck by a family's embarrassed children; amusingly, the film's "soundtrack," distorted as if it were emanating from a hook-on drive-in speaker and crammed into one channel of the mix, is a slice of "Mariachi Suite," from Los Lobos' score for *Desperado*. The songs fire a barrage of Central American rhythms and styles, customized like an East Side ride. The music cautioned against any literalism on the listener's part: "Don't go figure, it's not about hip / You won't get it, it's a Latin trip."

Released in March 1999, *Dose* was succeeded by a club tour that found the four collaborators—augmented by drummer Cougar Estrada (who shortly joined Los Lobos as the band's full-time drummer) and violinist Lisa Germano, who also appeared as an opening act—veering through their off-kilter "Latin trip" under an onstage canopy of Christmas lights and paper lanterns, playing their lavender-moon music with a stripped-down magic.

- 14 -

IN THE MOUSE'S HOUSE

Disney, Hollywood Records,
This Time, and *Good Morning Aztlán*

In 1996, *Colossal Head* became the first album by Los Lobos released solely under the Warner Bros. Records logo, following seven previous releases over the course of a decade on the joint Slash/Warner imprint.

It was also the band's last record for the company.

In the early and mid-'90s, an intense, ugly, and very public power struggle had developed within Time Warner's Warner Music Group, pitting its chief executive, Robert Morgado—a former New York political operative with no music industry experience—against Warner Bros. Records chairman Mo Ostin, the label's corporate linchpin since the early '60s. Ostin had announced his resignation in late 1994, and Lenny Waronker, Ostin's protégé and the label's president, declined to take over his mentor's job and himself exited the company in 1995. That October, Ostin and Waronker were hired by DreamWorks SKG—the entertainment combine founded by Steven Spielberg, former Disney executive Jeffrey Katzenberg, and David Geffen—to head their new record division. Morgado had himself been ousted that May and replaced by Michael Fuchs, the former head of cable TV giant HBO.

Many in the business believed that the "suits" had triumphed, and Warner's days as an "artist's label" were evidently over. The departure of the label's long-term stewards filled many of its acts, including Los Lobos, with uncertainty and dread.

"Everything was upside-down in the industry," Pérez

remembers. "This whole corporate thing came in, and Lenny had left . . . Everything was changing so fast. With Warner's, it was, 'This doesn't feel like the same Warner Bros. anymore.' It didn't feel like we had the support that we used to. With Warner Bros. in the early years, we'd go out on the road and we'd see the local [promotion] reps, and these guys became our friends. They'd make sure the records were in the stores in their region. We didn't see much of that anymore. The machine of the record industry was changing tremendously.

"They didn't let us go—we asked to be released."

In October 1997, the *Los Angeles Times* Sunday music industry gossip column "Pop Eye" revealed Los Lobos' departure from Warner Bros., and said the band was weighing offers from DreamWorks (naturally), Rykodisc, and Interscope Records, which had recently departed the Warner fold after corporate conflict over its hardcore rap releases. However, the band was ultimately signed by Hollywood Records, the pop music arm of Walt Disney Studios.

On the music side, the House That Mickey Mouse Built was then best known as the conduit for soundtracks drawn from Disney's incredibly profitable animated features; in 1994–1995, the companion album for the box office smash *The Lion King* sold ten million copies. However, the Hollywood label—founded as a pop music enclave by Michael Eisner, then Disney's chief executive, in 1989—was viewed as something of an embarrassment in the music industry. By 1997, it had lost more than $150 million; it had been unable to develop any meaningful acts of its own, and had seen its greatest success in the relaunch of the glammy U.K. rock act Queen's back catalog. Though management stabilized in 1998 with the hiring of Bob Cavallo, formerly the manager of Prince, to lead the newly minted Buena Vista Music Group (an umbrella for all Disney's imprints), Hollywood Records was still a commercial question mark that had hemorrhaged money for nearly a decade.

"When we signed to Hollywood Records, there was kind of a nebulous power structure there," Berlin recalls. "[At Warner Bros.] there was always this sense of, we knew Lenny, Lenny knew us, he knew this was gonna work or this wasn't gonna work. That certainty of the relationship didn't exist at Hollywood—[the label didn't have] a clear identity, and we didn't know who our boss was, or who we were working for, who was gonna be the guy who said 'yes' and 'no.'"

Despite the new environment, the decision was made to reunite Los Lobos with the team of Mitchell Froom and Tchad Blake. Today, Froom admits with admirable candor that the relationship between the co-producers and the band was beginning to suffer from fatigue, and that the on-the-fly methodology applied to *Colossal Head* and the two Latin Playboys albums didn't bear great fruit at Hollywood.

"Something was starting to wear out a little bit," he says. "It felt like that in the room. Everyone wasn't just dying to get to work every day. And maybe that affected my view of it. Quite a few things I remember really liking, but it didn't seem like it had the same drive. It almost seemed like it would have been better if they had come in with all written songs. It was getting to be a bit of a strain to have so much come together in the studio. That's my memory of it. It was always fun working with them . . . [But] it felt like something that was starting to run out of gas."

Also, the label's senior vice president of A&R, Rob Cavallo—Bob Cavallo's son, and a hit-making veteran of the talent department at Warner Bros., where he had signed Green Day and the Goo Goo Dolls—was interested in something Los Lobos hadn't delivered in a decade: a radio hit. For all the nearly universal critical respect accorded them, the band hadn't released a single that had even glanced off the chart since 1987, the year of "La Bamba."

Froom remembers, "[Rob] said, 'Well, it might be good if we had something that'll get us on the radio. It might be a helpful thing.' He wasn't heavy-handed. Then they played him some stuff, and what they played him was basically one-chord grooves with no singing on them. He said, 'I like all those. Work on that.' Then David went away and wrote 'This Time.' I don't think there was a lot of enthusiasm."

"We felt like 'This Time' was as close to a single as we were ever going to do in that era," says Berlin. "We were on a label that was more about the hits than Warner Bros. ever was . . . We shipped the song to radio and they [said], '*Eehhh* . . .' I think we were a little bit beat down by that—the fact that they didn't think that song was particularly special."

The album *This Time* became Los Lobos' Hollywood Records debut in July 1999. It's an uneasy mating of the spirited approach of *Kiko* and *Colossal Head* with an uncertain groping for a commercial hit; though it may not have been intentional on the part of the participants, almost everything on the record sounds slightly compromised, and even a little spooked. There are tracks to admire—the rolling, blissed-out title song; "Oh Yeah," a percolating collaborative surprise with a swerving, time-traveling story line by Rosas and Pérez; "Viking," a slamming recollection of an East Side *vato* penned by Pérez and Hidalgo; and "Cumbia Raza," a full-bore exploration of the swaying titular *ritmo* that was fast becoming Rosas's songwriting signature.

However, as the album's final track, a pile-up of frenetic rhythm and dissonant saxophones called "Why We Wish," collapses in a farrago of noise, feedback, and tape dropouts, the terminus of Los Lobos' theretofore brilliantly productive partnership with Froom and Blake is writ large on the wall.

"I could not be prouder of the work we did with Mitchell and Tchad," says Berlin. "I think that they are absolute, positive geniuses. I learned more from them than from anybody I've ever worked with. I respect them as highly as I can probably respect anybody at any level that I've met during my career. But it was a played-out string by the end of that record. We'd done everything that we could do . . . They'd probably say the same thing. It wasn't any of our best work. It certainly paled by comparison to what came before."

This Time peaked at No. 135 on the U.S. album chart, where it spent only three weeks.

~~~~~~

Tracks from *This Time* appeared on *El Cancionero Mas y Mas*, a four-CD, eighty-six-song Los Lobos retrospective released by

Warner Archives/Rhino Records in November 2000. The compilation, accompanied by a seventy-six-page booklet including three historical essays and a track-by-track analysis by Louie Pérez and critic Don Waller, surveyed the band's body of work dating back to "the yellow album," *Just Another Band from East L.A.*

The collection was dedicated to the memory of Cesar Rosas's wife, Sandra. In October 1999, while Los Lobos were on tour in the South, she was abducted from the family's Rowland Heights home by her half brother Gabriel Gomez, who killed her and buried her body in a Santa Clarita canyon. In October of 2000 Gomez was found guilty of kidnapping and first-degree murder and sentenced to life in prison without parole.

Los Lobos would not release a new record for two years.

～～～～～～～～～～～～～～～～～～～～～～～～～～～～～～

When the time came for the band to enter the studio again, they were reassigned to another imprint under the Hollywood Records umbrella: Mammoth Records. Originally based in Carrboro, North Carolina, the label—home to such valued indie acts as the Squirrel Nut Zippers (a Chapel Hill band whose 1997 album *Hot* had been a platinum-selling hit), Joe Henry, Jason & the Scorchers, and Juliana Hatfield—had been founded by entrepreneur Jay Faires in 1989 and acquired by Disney in 1998.

What looked like a promising arrangement swiftly soured, according to Hidalgo: "Jay Faires was the only one who knew anything about the band. We thought, 'OK, this sounds like a good deal, we'll get some personal attention.' Then, just before our record came out, they closed down Mammoth, and he left the company. 'All right, *great*.' It was not a good place to be."

While it was decided that a new album could be economically recorded at Rosas's home studio, CRG, the band was asked to work with a new co-producer.

"The record company said, 'We need a name,'" says Pérez. "They brought in John Leckie."

Leckie arrived in Rowland Heights bearing a heavy-duty résumé. He had begun his career at EMI's legendary Abbey Road facility, engineering such albums as John Lennon's *Plastic Ono Band*, George Harrison's *All Things Must Pass*, Pink Floyd's *Meddle*, and Paul McCartney's *Red Rose Speedway*. After cutting his teeth as a producer with a series of albums by Bill Nelson's fiery, guitar-centric band Be Bop Deluxe, he worked with a succession of top-flight British acts: Simple Minds, XTC, Magazine, the Stone Roses, Radiohead, and the Verve.

However, though the Lobos today evince nothing but admiration for Leckie personally, they confess that—perhaps because of an insurmountable cultural gulf between the British producer and the Chicano musicians—he brought little to the table during his sessions with them.

"He was a really good guy," Berlin says, "but he was, I think, somewhat intimidated by us, and once we got him in the studio he was afraid to do much."

"John Leckie was a real cool guy, but he didn't do anything," Pérez claims. "We made that record ourselves. He's a wonderful man, but he wasn't a real proactive dude . . . John wasn't really present creatively. It was, 'Oh, yeah, that's cool.'"

"He was just kinda there," says Rosas. "We'd ask, 'Is it a take?' And he'd go, 'What do you guys think?'"

Ultimately, says Berlin, Leckie "wasn't fired, but he got kinda sent home. We mixed almost the entire record with [engineer] Dave McNair, and then finished [recording] the record with Dave, because John had gone back to England." (The band took sole production credit on three of the album's twelve tracks.)

The finished product, *Good Morning Aztlán*, appeared in June 2002 as a nearly complete departure from the risky, off-center albums Los Lobos had formulated with Froom and Blake. Largely lacking either the rootsy orientation of the band's first records or the manic try-anything energy of their '90s work, it's for the most part a loud, purposelessly busy guitar album that, absent its occasional Spanish lyrics and *cumbia* outbursts, could have been the work of any rock band. Some of its songs—the convulsive title track and "Done Gone Blue"—would prove to be sturdy concert cornerstones, but the writing for the most part could not be accused of distinction. An exception: "Luz de Mi

Vida," a rare Rosas–Pérez co-write, which can be interpreted as Rosas's poignant farewell to his late wife.

"[The album] sounds like it was kind of slapped together," Pérez admits. "It was one of the few times we felt like they were asking us for a hit. It didn't feel good, and Dave and I went back and wrote that song called 'Round & Round,' which I really don't like. It felt really forced. They literally twisted our arms to get that song out of us."

In the wake of *Good Morning Aztlán*'s attenuated recording and disappointing performance (it peaked at No. 82 and lasted five weeks on the *Billboard* album chart), Los Lobos decided they would produce their records themselves in the future.

"On all of the records, we had a big part of the production," Hidalgo says. "Some of the stuff we would end up finishing ourselves anyway. So we said, 'Well, why pay somebody thirty grand to do something that we can do ourselves?'"

"We'd finally just had it," says Rosas. "We finally said, 'No more, man. That's it.'"

- 15 -

HOMECOMINGS

The Ride, The Town and the City,
Tin Can Trust

In 2003, Los Lobos marked their thirtieth year together. They had commemorated their twentieth anniversary in 1993 with the release of a two-CD retrospective—titled, like their folk debut, *Just Another Band from East L.A.*—but 2000's box *El Cancionero Mas y Mas* left another such gambit out of the question.

Instead, the band decided to reconsider their three-decade career via a new studio album—a collection of both new and old material interpreted in tandem with some of the performers whose work had left an impression on their own. Says Hidalgo, "We thought, well, it'd be nice to [do] kind of a tribute, as a thank-you to the people that we admired and the people that meant a lot to us throughout the years."

"One day," Berlin remembers, "we literally sat down and wrote down everybody we could think of that we liked. Then we crossed off all the dead guys—there were probably fifteen of those. So then we were down to twenty or so. Then it was: Who would really matter? Who could we do something with that would be significant and cool and important? So we started to just call people . . . and almost every single person that we asked said yes."

Some of the performers on what became *The Ride* hailed from the Lobos' own backyard. Thee Midniters' Little Willie G., whose 2000 HighTone solo album *Make Up for the Lost Time* had been produced by Hidalgo, was drafted to sing a new version of "Is This All There Is?"

The singer recalls, "They asked me, 'Hey, are you free? We're meeting over at Cesar's house. Do you have *By the Light of the Moon*?' I told them I was familiar with it. When I got to Cesar's, they were all set up and ready for me to record my vocals. It was one of those [instances of] living up to my reputation—'Two-Take Willie.' They were happy with what I did. We did two takes, and they said they'd take it from there."

An appearance by Dave Alvin entailed the recording of the first song co-written by the Blasters' former principal tunesmith with Pérez and Hidalgo.

"There was a discussion about, well, should we do a cover, or something of mine," Alvin says. "And they said maybe we can write something together . . . This was right after my dad had died, and it was right after the whole issue with Sandra [Rosas], the discovery of her body, all this sort of sad, uncomfortable stuff. And then [there was] the larger picture of other people who had passed away. So we got on the topic of mourning, so that was the genesis of the song. We batted it around for a couple of nights.

"I did say, 'Hey, if it's a really good song, I'm gonna use it on my record.' They said, 'That's fine by us.'"

As a result, the moving "Somewhere in Time" appeared on both *The Ride* and Alvin's 2004 solo album *Ashgrove*; the gifted guitarist Greg Leisz, who is heard on both versions, produced Alvin's rendition.

A folk–rock ballad about a maritime disaster was custom-tailored for the English singer–guitarist Richard Thompson, whose work with Fairport Convention had been such a formative influence on Hidalgo and Pérez.

"We knew 'The Wreck of the Carlos Rey' was going to be a song for Richard Thompson," Pérez says, "and I really liked the idea that I was going to write a line that I was going to hear Richard Thompson sing in Spanish. I got a kick out of that. I wrote it for that reason."

The Latin aspect of the band's work was represented by two songs entirely in Spanish: "La Venganza de Los Pelados," a swaggering number co-written by Hidalgo, Pérez, and Luis Torres and performed with the Mexican rock band Café Tacuba, and the swaying "Ya Se Va," written by Rosas and Hidalgo with the Panamanian salsa star Ruben Blades.

"He's a bad dude, man," Lozano says of Blades. "He came over to Cesar's house, to the studio. He came in, we showed him what to do, and he did it in two takes, man. That was it. That was all he needed. He was done in forty-five minutes. He did such an amazing job."

"We made it easy for everyone," says Hidalgo. "We wanted it to be fun for the people who agreed to do it. We asked Elvis Costello if he would be interested in doing a version of 'A Matter of Time.' He said, 'Yeah, but I'm on tour.' So we said, 'However you want to do it.' So he recorded it at a soundcheck in Norway. That's the version that's on the album—we added the harmony part and put Greg Leisz on it, and that was it. Mavis Staples was in Chicago, so when we were out that way, we stopped in and recorded her [singing "Someday"] so she wouldn't have to travel.

"We asked Tom Waits if he'd be interested in doing it, and he said, 'Yeah, I'll do it, but I want to record it on cassette.' So it was recorded on cassette. He wanted his part on cassette, too. We sent him a track on cassette, and he added vocals. He also said, 'I want to sing in Spanish.' So he came up with 'Kitate.'"

The album's longest track, and its musical high point, is R&B singer–guitarist Bobby Womack's appearance on an eight-minute medley of Rosas's doomy *Kiko* composition "Wicked Rain"—which had originally been inspired by some intensive listening to Womack's music—and "Across 110th Street," Womack's memorable theme for the like-titled 1972 crime picture. Womack plays elegant acoustic guitar on the track, and duets with Rosas.

"It was fucking surreal to me," Rosas remembers with a delighted laugh. "I couldn't believe it. I was playing with *Bobby Womack*! We had sent him a demo of the song. When I met him in the studio, I told him, 'You are the reason why this song came together. We recorded it a certain way. But how about this?' And I played it to him in a more soulful way, the way it was intended to be."

Relaxed and brimming with warmth and a real sense of fun, *The Ride* was the most direct and purely entertaining music from Los Lobos since the band's earliest Slash recordings. Much of the album's charm emanates from the Lobos' self-effacing approach to the material. Most million-selling acts would celebrate three decades in business by flexing their egos; Los Lobos carved their milestone by essentially serving as a backup band.

Pérez says, "It did sound like we were the house band . . . It was kind of like we had a party for our thirtieth anniversary. The next morning you get up and pick up all of the empties and sweep everything out, and it becomes just another day."

Lofted by significant press coverage of the anniversary, *The Ride* was supported simultaneously by the release of *Ride This*, a rough-hewn EP containing the Lobos' covers of seven songs written or originated by Womack, Costello, Blades, Thompson, Alvin, and (with Thee Midniters) Garcia (Willie G.). The album attained the group's highest chart position since *La Bamba*, reaching No. 75. Though not a hit, it served as a reminder that Los Lobos were still making heartfelt music that streamed from a dozen musical tributaries.

It may have been coincidental, but some of Los Lobos' finest latter-day music was created immediately on the heels of the breathtaking 2005–2006 concerts in which the group performed *Kiko* in its entirety. Though the band had played the majority of the music off the album on tour in 1992–1993 when it was new, the record had since attained the status of a classic, and the band essayed it from start to finish for the first time in a series of club and theater shows more than a decade later.

For whatever reason, the band's music jelled brilliantly in the thematically linked songs written by Hidalgo and Pérez for the album that succeeded the *Kiko* shows.

Hidalgo says, "I had a box of all the cassettes I'd recorded. Before we went in the studio, I went through them, and I found some ideas that I thought were worth working on, even if they were little short things . . . Quite a few of those songs were cassette demos that we ended up using. It came together in the studio. One good thing about writing songs like that is if the songs come from the same period of time, they're linked somehow. They have a similar feel. They seem to fit together. It started to feel like that—almost like a concept record."

"We started thinking about our parents," Pérez continues. "I was having conversations with Dave about my mom, and his mom. We started thinking about what our parents had to go through to get over here. Then it started to widen beyond my own experience.

"[The album] starts with 'The Valley'—almost like a creation myth—then it moves from 'The Road to Gila Bend,' with the guys coming across the border, and then it lands in the middle with 'The City,' where this person is being almost overwhelmed by his new life, and then somehow he makes his way to the very end, back to 'The Town.' That record is about East L.A., and about the place where we all came from. It's almost like this big circle. The way the record's been sequenced, with a beginning, a middle, and an end, it's like a book."

Pérez acknowledges that the title of the album, released under a joint Hollywood/Mammoth logo as *The Town and the City* in September 2006, is a nod to Jack Kerouac's like-titled first novel, published in 1950.

Not only did the record sport a strong and powerful narrative through-line, but it was sonically refreshed as well. Nine of the album's thirteen tracks were mixed by Tchad Blake, returning to the wolf pack after a seven-year absence. His fingerprints are apparent from the first trembling backward guitar lines that ripple through the album-opening "The Valley."

The Town and the City is an album of darkness and fleeting light. Its key tracks are harrowing—"The Road to Gila Bend" (a depiction of a fearful illegal immigrant's run across the border that is a close thematic cousin to the band's early breakthrough "A Matter of Time"), "The City" (a somber promise to "shoot out all the neon lights" of downtown L.A.), "The Town" (a foreboding pastoral seething with the threat of inexplicable violence).

In the record's perilous universe, even material success offers no succor: the wealthy self-made man of "Little Things," a towering Hidalgo ballad performance that melodically calls to mind "A Whiter Shade of Pale," has gained the world but lost his soul. A cloud of desperation hangs over the record; it is felt to its fullest in the lyrics to "Hold On":

> *Hold on*
> *Hold on to every breath*
> *And if I make it to the sunrise*
> *Just to do it all over again*
> *Do it all over again*
> *I'm killing myself just to keep alive*
> *Killing myself to survive*
> *Killing myself to survive*

In keeping with its autobiographically grounded nature, the album includes three songs in Spanish (one of them, the comparatively sunny "Luna," a rare performance *en Español* by Hidalgo, who also contributes a beautiful solo on the Cuban *tres*); Cesar responds with two of his brightest compositions, the homeboy anthem "Chuco's Cumbia" and an offbeat slice of Latin reggae, "No Puedo Mas." No matter what the material, the band plays it with tremendous assurance, and with no showboating; it is a skilled and unshowy ensemble performance, with all hands carefully serving the skillfully penned songs. Like *Kiko*, it feels all of a brilliant piece. By any measure, it plays like a late-career masterwork.

To the band's horror, despite some glowing reviews, *The Town and the City* was a nearly complete commercial failure. Its somber tone may have kept listeners from embracing it. It topped out at No. 142 on the charts, and to date has sold only fifty thousand copies, according to figures from the music sales metrics firm Nielsen SoundScan.

"It was overlooked, to a painful degree," says Pérez. "I know David was really hurt that it didn't get any attention. It was so disappointing for us. For Dave and myself, it was like, 'We can never do *Kiko* again—however those planets lined up, it's not going to happen. But this is an incredible simulation.'"

~~~~~~

In the wake of the dismal commercial performance of *The Town and the City*, the band was angry, and they felt they had only Disney's music division to blame.

"That was so disappointing," Pérez says. "It was handed to them, as they say, on a silver platter. The press was behind it. And they did nothing with it to promote it.

"We knew we had one more record to do [for Hollywood Records] and we didn't want to do a studio record [of new material] . . . We actually approached them saying, 'We don't want to do another studio record, we'd like to do another children's record.' They countered that by saying, 'If you want to do another children's record, you can do Disney songs.' We said, 'OK, we'll figure it out.'"

Another children's record was not a stretch for the group that had received a Grammy nod for *Papa's Dream*. Additionally, Los Lobos had already proved that they could hit a home run with a song from the Disney canon: their version of "I Wan'na Be Like You," a capering number originally sung by Louis Prima for the 1967 animated feature *The Jungle Book*, had been a spunky highlight of *Stay Awake*, an offbeat 1988 recital of Disney songs produced by Hal Willner for A&M.

Alas, the band's collective heart was clearly not in the making of the awkwardly titled *Los Lobos Goes Disney*, eventually released (if that is the proper word) in 2009 on Disney Sound, a short-lived imprint that was essentially a venue for children's music by the two-man alternative rock group They Might Be Giants. The set might as well have been titled *Los Lobos Fulfill Their Contract*. It is carelessly produced and indifferently sung and played. The repertoire, which included a couple of numbers derived from theme park rides, is unusually dull and unimaginative. (It even contains a sluggish remake of "I Wan'na Be Like You.") Only a Lobos fan interested in "It's a

Small World" rendered as a border polka or a Spanish version of "Heigh-Ho" would find it compelling. *Los Lobos Goes Disney* became the band's only studio album to miss the charts completely, and the worst-selling release of their major-label career; according to SoundScan, it had sold less than nine thousand copies as of April 2014.

~~~~~~

The Aztec calendar is round, and with their departure from the Disney fold Los Lobos found that over time they had gone in something of a circle themselves. They were in a position they hadn't encountered for twenty-six years: they were without the services of a major record label.

"We were without a label for a long time," says Pérez. "There was nobody urging us along to make another record. A lot of time went by just touring. Finally we decided to make another record. There were a number of labels we were looking at, and Shout! Factory made the most sense."

Launched by Richard Foos, the co-founder of Rhino Records, Shout! Factory is a Sony-distributed, independently operated imprint that, like its precursor, issued a plethora of boomer-friendly back-catalog material on CD and DVD, with an emphasis on music. The company maintained only a small roster of contemporary talent, and the Lobos were probably the label's most prominent act. Unlike their previous albums, which were funded by Warner Bros. and Disney and became a permanent part of the labels' catalogs, the band's new release was recorded by the band itself and licensed to Shout! Factory. Given that even their debut album, *Just Another Band from East L.A.*, was made under the New Vista Productions banner, Los Lobos were now in a sense truly independent for the first time in their recording career.

After more than a decade of making records at Cesar Rosas's home facility, the guitarist had moved and the band no longer had access to a studio. The group's engineer Shane Smith had worked at small, funky Manny's Estudio in the heart of East L.A. and recommended it to Steve Berlin. Sessions for the new record commenced there, with the band recording together as a unit in one room, face-to-face and live.

Lozano recalls, "The place we did it at, this kind of beat-up East L.A. studio, was a good place to play and hang out and record these songs . . . We went in there with nothing and put it all together as we went."

A shortage of material again proved to be a challenge.

"It was the most difficult writing process that ever happened," Pérez remembers. "We usually set aside a month or six weeks or so to work on our new songs, and we'd usually come up with a half dozen songs and go into the studio, and that kind of kick-started it. We get into it enough where we're actually writing as we're recording. We'd usually have something to prime the pump. We had three weeks or a month or whatever to write, and during that period it was like, 'Hey, Dave, you got something?' 'Uhh, I thought *you* did.' It went on and on and on, and we didn't have anything . . . I was literally digging into some stuff that I'd had for awhile, and Dave did, too, bits and pieces of stuff, some stuff from *The Town and the City* . . . But I love that record. It's about being back in the neighborhood again."

The album that was finally released as *Tin Can Trust* in August 2010 does contain some makeweight material. "Do the Murray" is a Freddie King–styled instrumental that gives both Hidalgo and Rosas a chance to show off their blues chops. The set's longest track, the seven-minute "West L.A. Fadeaway," is a cover of a song from the Grateful Dead's hugely popular 1987 album *In the Dark*, and serves as an expansive homage to the San Francisco band that the Lobos first opened for in 1988 (and whose "Bertha" they had covered on the 1991 tribute album *Deadicated*).

Of the album's nine other songs, three were Rosas's; besides the obligatory *cumbia* "Yo Canto" and the Tex–Mex polka "Mujer Ingrata," the guitarist made another Dead connection by collaborating with the San Francisco band's longtime lyricist Robert Hunter for an intensely played ballad, "All My Bridges Burning." Despite their struggle with the writing process, Pérez and Hidalgo responded with a few noteworthy compositions:

the title track, which combined a slippery melody with an on-the-skids narrative that played like a latter-day complement to "Angels with Dirty Faces"; "The Lady and the Rose," a folk-inclined ballad that reflects the enormous impact of Richard Thompson's work on the two songwriters; and the album-closing "27 Spanishes," a darkly comic account of a sixteenth-century encounter between the Aztecs and a platoon of their Spanish conquerors-to-be that rides a sardonic, turned-around beat.

Despite the difficulty of its birthing, *Tin Can Trust* was reviewed favorably and became the first Los Lobos album to reach the Top 50 in thirty-three years. It peaked at No. 47, matching the top chart positions of both *How Will the Wolf Survive?* and *By the Light of the Moon*.

EPILOGUE

40: Back at the Whisky

In September 2013, Los Lobos announced that they would be doing a handful of intimate shows commemorating their fortieth anniversary, including one at the Whisky a Go Go on Hollywood's Sunset Strip, the site of the band's first high-profile gig outside East L.A. The anniversary bill was sweetened by the opening act: the Blasters, for whom the Lobos had themselves opened at that now-storied 1981 show. Fans snapped up the tickets within hours.

The announcement of the show prefaced by a month the release of the concert recording *Disconnected in New York*, the band's first album issued through the Los Angeles indie imprint 429 Records. Not entirely unplugged but acoustic-based and decidedly low-key, it was the band's fifth concert album in nine years. *Live at the Fillmore*, recorded at the titular San Francisco venue that is one of the Lobos' homes away from home, had been issued on CD and DVD by Hollywood Records in 2005; the repertoire leaned heavily on their latter-day albums. In 2012, in conjunction with the twentieth-anniversary reissue of *Kiko*, Shout! Factory tardily issued the CD and DVD *Kiko Live*, captured at San Diego's House of Blues during the brief 2005–2006 tour of the album. Additionally, the band itself issued the self-descriptive *Acoustic En Vivo* and two volumes of live performances titled *One Time One Night*.

Increasingly, this was an act that was living onstage; their 2012–2013 itinerary had included North American and European dates opening for Neil Young and a run of package shows with their *hermanos* Los Lonely Boys and Alejandro Escovedo. Now they were returning to the venue where they had given a breakthrough performance.

On November 14, the night of the Whisky show, I put on my most comfortable shoes and headed to the club. I expected to see some people I knew there, and I was not disappointed: walking up to a small queue in front of the club, I immediately ran into photographer Joel Aparicio, newly returned from Texas; his sister Stella Aparicio Perez, that devoted follower of the band since their earliest days, and her husband; and Stella's friend and fellow fan Susan Spencer. All of them had been fixtures of the band's early Hollywood shows, and had remained ardent fans; I had seen Stella and Susan literally dancing in the aisles at the first Los Lobos Festival at the Greek.

When the time came to file into the club, I entered apprehensively. I had last been in the Whisky in 2006 for another commemorative date: an invitation-only affair launching *Perception*, a newly remastered collection of the studio albums by another act that had made its name at the Whisky forty years before, the Doors. It had been a dispiriting affair. Owing to very public differences between the surviving members, Ray Manzarek and Robby Krieger had held court at the venue, while John Densmore performed on a hand drum in exile at Book Soup, a bookstore two blocks up the Strip.

My presence at the Whisky for the Doors' promotional evening had been a rare visit to a club that had been a second home to me in the late '70s and early '80s. It had closed in 1982, and when it reopened four years later its somewhat seedy allure had degenerated into a kind of threadbare utility. It skidded further as time went on. Its leatherette booths were ripped out, the friendly old staff scattered, and the vibe that had made the club a magnet for top talent dissipated completely. The room had also pioneered "pay to play" shows, a risk-free gambit for the venue (often mounted by independent promoters who "four walled" the night), in which naive young bands purchased tickets to their dates and resold them to their fans, friends, and family. This extortionate practice has persisted to this day; it is not uncommon to look up at the old rock showplace's big, bright marquee at the corner of Sunset and Clark and see the names of six or seven bands, all of them unknown, and likely to remain so. (A brief respite from the usual fare came in January 2014, when the Gray Lady of the Strip celebrated its own fiftieth anniversary with a month of shows by name attractions that had once graced the club, including X.)

I was expecting the worst when I walked through the door, but was immediately cheered to discover I was in a club I recognized. In fact, the Whisky resembled its old self so greatly that I momentarily experienced a sensation of time travel. The booths on the club's west wall had been restored; while it was unlikely that the label vice presidents and rock high-rollers who had reveled there in the joint's heyday would ever sit in them again, it was warming to see them back in their Naugahyde glory. The place, which had been dingy and sometimes foul-smelling in later years, appeared to have acquired a new coat of paint. Tables again lined the railings on the narrow second level, and the downstairs and upstairs bars bustled. There was no reason to believe that the club would return to the prominence of its glory days—which were commemorated in a portrait of Jim Morrison and other Doors artifacts hanging on the club's south wall—but some of the great old dive's flavor had been reinstated.

There still didn't appear to be enough waitresses—some things hadn't changed since back in the day—but they would have been thwarted soon enough anyway. As showtime approached, the dance floor filled up with a mixture of *veteranos* both brown and white, their hair silvery, many of the men wearing Los Lobos concert shirts of varying vintages, the women dressier in outfits suitable for dancing, some understated, some elegant. Some younger patrons were present, too—many of them in the company of what looked to be their parents—seeking a taste of what they hadn't been around to experience three decades before.

At the stroke of 8:00 p.m., the Blasters—founding members Phil Alvin, bassist John Bazz, and drummer Bill Bateman, with guitarist Keith Wyatt, a member since 1996—took the stage to a flood of warm applause. Inhaling the nostalgia that was thick in the air, they kicked off their set with "Flattop Joint," a Dave Alvin song that dated back to the group's 1980 Rollin' Rock debut album, which had so impressed Los Lobos.

After four songs, Wyatt was displaced by Dave Alvin, who strode onstage in a cowboy hat to a roar from the audience and took his place at his older brother Phil's elbow. At that juncture, the frequently contentious siblings still appeared together on stage with relative rarity, but Dave and Phil had grown close again after the elder Alvin had a brush with death during a June 2012 European tour. (In 2014, the Alvins would tour together nationally behind their collaborative recital of Big Bill Broonzy songs, *Common Ground*.)

A succession of old Blasters crowd-pleasers—songs that had inspired Los Lobos' earliest compositions—followed: "Red Rose," "Trouble Bound," "American Music," "Border Radio," and "Marie Marie" (the latter of which Phil, who now almost invariably sings it in Spanish, essayed in a rare English version). For the climactic "One Bad Stud," the unit, with Wyatt again in the fold, was joined by Steve Berlin, returning to his old role to blow a spirited baritone sax chorus. As the fans cheered and the other band members moved up the stairs to the dressing room, Phil and Dave paused for a second at the center of the stage, and Dave wrapped his arm around his brother's shoulder, beaming in bliss.

With Los Lobos' set imminent, the dance floor was even more tightly packed than it had been earlier in the evening; after escaping for a smoke and a stop at the bar for a couple of bottled waters, I had to slowly wedge myself back to my former position near the front of the stage. Then a howl went up as Los Lobos del Este de Los Angeles, the pride of the East Side, paused for a moment on the landing above the stairs leading to the stage.

The band took their places as my eyes darted around the club. I momentarily lost sight of Louie Pérez, and from my vantage point the drum kit was partially blocked by an amplifier. It was only when I saw drummer Bugs Gonzalez crouching next to the drums that I realized Pérez had taken his old chair; he would pound the skins for the first five songs in the set, for old times' sake.

Clarion notes from David Hidalgo's gold accordion kicked off "Anselma." At the song's conclusion, Cesar Rosas, taking the master of ceremonies role he has commanded since the band's Hollywood ascent, exclaimed, "Thank God that we're still here! I've got a lot of blurry memories." Then, with a dedication to their late, longtime roadie Mouse de la Luz, who had died in January, they bounded into the early-'80s bopper "Let's Say Goodnight." They next essayed a pair of oldies familiar to any East Side *vato*: the requisite Ritchie Valens cover "That's My Little Suzie," and Bo Diddley's slow-grinding "I'm Sorry." "That's some pachuco music right there," said Rosas.

After taking out the mini-set of way-back numbers with a bopping "Why Do You Do," Bugs Gonzalez finally claimed the drum seat, while Pérez stepped to his now-customary position at center stage. He momentarily took up the *jarana* for the acoustic "La Venganza de Los Pelados" (with a rare Spanish-language vocal by David Hidalgo), then strapped on an electric guitar for Rosas's bluesy "My Baby's Gone," a somber "The Valley," "Chuco's Cumbia," and "Chains of Love." The crowd swayed as the band slipped into "Kiko," the night's mystical moment.

Again warming the old-timers in the crowd, Pérez retook the drum stool for a couple of sturdy Chicano flag-wavers. "Mexicano Americano," a brown-pride statement penned by Texan Rumel Fuentes, is seldom heard in the Lobos' sets. The band probably first heard it in Los Pinguinos del Norte's version on the soundtrack of *Chulas Fronteras*, Les Blank's 1979 documentary about border music, and Rosas dueted with Alejandro Escovedo on a version that appeared on *By the Hand of the Father*, the 2002 companion to Escovedo's like-titled autobiographical play. The other number was instantly recognizable to the crowd: a *grito* went up as the band ground into the slow drag of "Volver, Volver," a core component of the Lobos' repertoire even before the band's Whisky bow. Many in the crowd bellowed the chorus, and a handful of couples ground against each other in the crush of the dance floor.

Pérez returned to guitar, for it was time to rock the formal set to a close. With a nod to their spiritual forebears, the band essayed the Dead's "West L.A. Fadeaway" (after a query from Cesar: "Do we have any Jerry's kids?"), then closed with a surging trifecta of Little Bob's "I Got Loaded," "Don't Worry Baby," and an elongated "Mas y Mas," with full-force solos by Hidalgo and Pérez.

The noisy crowd would not let Los Lobos escape without an encore, and the band climbed down from the dressing room again for a rip at "Evangeline" and a cover of Johnny Thunders's "Alone in a Crowd," with Pérez handling both lead vocal and lead guitar chores, as he had on a 1994 Thunders tribute album released in Japan.

Certain inevitabilities remain at Lobos shows of special import, and many were no doubt waiting for another Valens tune to conclude the night. So it was a surprise to some when Hidalgo and the band launched into the unmistakable chords of Bob Dylan's "Like a Rolling Stone." But then David stepped to the mic and began to seamlessly sing: *"La la la la la bamba, necessita una poca de gracia ... "* There it was: the mash-up known as "Like a Rolling Bamba," concocted in the late '90s as an alternative to playing The Hit for the thousandth time, now performed in all its raging glory, capped with a long solo from Rosas.

The audience could have asked for more, but didn't. It had been an exhausting retrospective, especially for the large number of fifty- and sixtysomethings in attendance. Many in the house, some of whom had been seeing Los Lobos perform for the better part of their four decades in business, were probably feeling as worn out as I did. My feet were sore, my knees ached, my back rippled with pain, and my throat was slightly raw from cheering.

Nonetheless, I ventured upstairs to see if I could visit the band for a minute, but the Whisky's beefy security men, some of whom were probably toddlers when Los Lobos first played the club, appeared disinclined to allow anyone without an after-show pass to enter the sanctum—especially a gray-haired man well beyond fighting trim.

No matter, I thought to myself as I headed for the street. I'll see them again soon. Four decades on, Los Lobos abide.

As this book was going to press, Los Lobos was completing recording sessions for a new studio album at Blue Velvet Recording Studio in Santa Ana, California.

GRACIAS VERY MUCH

I've known the founding members of Los Lobos since 1982; my friendship with Steve Berlin predated his arrival in the group by a couple of years. Cesar, David, Louie, Conrad, and Steve have always been welcoming to this nosy gringo, and have maintained their patience over the course of several decades.

This book is not an authorized work; the band never asked to see a word of the text. They also never attempted to deter me from probing them about a topic that might be uncomfortable. I'm grateful for their candor, and for their willingness to cover a lot of old ground, some of which was not always pleasant to survey.

I'd also like to thank the Lobos again for playing my wedding in 1983. I hope this work does their extraordinary career some justice.

Special thanks are due Francisco González, who shed an important and irreplaceable shaft of light on the band's story with incredible frankness and honesty. He has heretofore received insufficient credit for playing the critical role in the birth of Los Lobos.

In addition to the interviews conducted for this book in 2012–2014, I drew from my earlier chats with the band for *Spin* (1985) and *Tower Pulse* (1996), as well as conversations for the 2000 Rhino boxed set *El Cancionero Mas y Mas*.

I must acknowledge the editors I worked with in my alternative-weekly days—James Vowell, Natalie Nichols, Steve

Appleford, John Payne, and Rebecca Schoenkopf. The stories I wrote for them about Los Lobos, the Blasters, and Little Willie G. in the *Los Angeles Reader*, *L.A. Weekly*, and *Los Angeles City-Beat* all came into play during the writing of this book. Gratitude also goes to Cynthia Littleton, my longtime editor at the *Hollywood Reporter* and *Variety*.

This project could not have been completed without the assistance of Gene Aguilera. I met Gene at one of the innumerable Lobos shows I attended in the '80s, and he has been a beloved brother ever since. His devotion to the Lobos was and remains fanatical, and he has an enormous archive of clippings, memorabilia, and rare audio and video that he opened for my use. Gene's own efforts to document the unknown history of the East Side's music have been covered in the *Los Angeles Times* and *L.A. Weekly* and on National Public Radio. He is also the author of *Mexican American Boxing in Los Angeles* (Arcadia Publishing, 2014), a look into another important element of East L.A. culture. *Gracias, carnale.*

A couple of other old friends, Joel Aparicio and his sister Stella Aparicio Perez, served up some very useful info about Los Lobos' early days in Hollywood.

Thank God for the Internet, and especially for Dan Gale's LobosBase, the Lobos fan site The Neighborhood, and Mark-Guerrero.com, the info-packed site run by Lalo Guerrero's son (Garfield High class of 1967).

For their efforts in helping me get my foot in several doors, I thank Los Lobos' road manager Mando Tavares, Larry Jenkins, Kevin Morris of Red Light Management, Tresa Redburn of Dept. 56, Lauren Gaffney-Blum of Shout! Factory, Vanessa Kromer of the Nederlander Organization, Tom Cording of Sony Legacy, and Kurt Nishimura of Silverlake Media.

My old *amigo* Bill Bentley and his *compadre* Joe Nick Patoski are a pair of great Texicans.

Bryan Thomas, who flacked for many years at Ritchie Valens's record label Del-Fi, graciously loaned me the original manuscript of his late boss Bob Keane's memoir *The Oracle of Del-Fi*, which Bryan hammered into shape for publication. Mike

Minky gave me an advance look at the invaluable notes for his label's *The Rampart Records Story*.

Essential chart information was supplied by Keith Caulfield of *Billboard*. *Grazie* to Rob McDonald for crunching some numbers for me, and for his friendship.

Several others pointed me in the right direction: Don Snowden, Art Fein, Gregg Sutton, Ric Ovalle, and David Hirshland of Bug Music.

Thanks to Tom Waits for being Tom Waits.

Likewise to Ruby Friedman for being Ruby Friedman.

Peter Blackstock, who co-edits the University of Texas Press American Music Series with another old colleague, David Menconi, contacted me in the spring of 2012 and asked me if I'd be interested in writing this book, thereby providing an answer to the question many have asked for years: "When are you gonna write a book, Morris?" Peter knew how close the subject was to my heart, and I ran with it.

Lastly, and most importantly, my gratitude and profound appreciation goes to my UT Press editor Casey Kittrell. His patience and professionalism during the writing of this book have been virtually infinite. Had it been *truly* infinite, you probably wouldn't be reading it now.

LISTENING, READING,
AND VIEWING

In the waning days of the compact disc, any discography is necessarily transitory. The CDs listed here are for those who still employ the format and are willing to do a little digging. Many of the titles should be available via online retailers like iTunes and Amazon (some of them in MP3 form), or through streaming services such as Spotify. Your author prefers to consume his music in the old-school fashion. A few long-out-of-print LPs are also discussed.

Traditional Mexican music is a bottomless pit, and there are certainly thousands of releases, both domestic and imported, that take in important material from south of the border. For English-speaking listeners, the best and most readily accessible passage into the music is via Chris Strachwitz's El Cerrito, California–based label Arhoolie Records. The company has issued many of the crucial vintage recordings of *tejano* and Tex–Mex *conjunto* music, including compilations devoted to Los Alegres de Teran and Flaco Jimenez, and you can find them at Arhoolie's website, Arhoolie.com. The label's Hispanic music catalog is largely drawn from Strachwitz's monumental archive of 130,000 discs; the book *The Arhoolie Foundation's Strachwitz Frontera Collection of Mexican and Mexican American Recordings*, published by UCLA's Chicano Studies Research Center, offers invaluable background. Arhoolie has also released a DVD of *Chulas Fronteras*, the late Les Blank's fabulous 1976 film about Tex–Mex and *norteño*; it includes footage of Los Alegres de Teran, the originators of "Anselma."

One Arhoolie volume that's a must is *Pachuco Boogie*, a 2002 compilation of the music that lit up the L.A. barrio in the late '40s and early '50s. It includes two versions of Don Tosti's groundbreaking titular hit, where Cali Hispanic culture and the swinging R&B boogie of popular black acts like Louis Jordan collided head-on. The set also includes pachuco-themed numbers formulated in styles ranging from traditional string bands to big band swing and bop. It is delicious.

Pachuco Boogie also includes three numbers by Los Lobos' future collaborator Lalo Guerrero, waxed during his pachuco epoch in the late '40s, backed by his working group, prophetically named Sus Cinco Lobos. Unfortunately, Lalo's scandalous hit "Marihuana Boogie" is not among those tracks; it can be heard on some Guerrero compilations that are hard to find outside of East L.A. record stores. My call is *The Original Chicano* (available from Original Chicano Productions, P.O. Box 261003, Los Angeles, CA 90026), which is packaged with an excellent biographical DVD and contains "There's No Tortillas," a parody of "O Solo Mio" cut with David Hidalgo and Conrad Lozano of Los Lobos and first released on the 1981 Ambiente album *Parodies of Lalo Guerrero*.

Leaping forward to the rock 'n' roll era, the complete works of Ritchie Valens were compiled on three CDs by Del-Fi Records in 1998 as *Come On, Let's Go*. Sadly out of print but still circulating at collector's prices, it is the one to get, despite the ready availability of various hits collections; my friend Bryan Thomas's notes for the boxed set supply deep history and context. The box includes all of Valens's studio material and his posthumously released live album *In Concert at Pacoima Jr. High*. The late Bob Keane's privately published 2005 memoir *The Oracle of Del-Fi*, which duplicates some of the material in the notes for the Valens box, offers the label owner's flavorful view of the Valens legend.

The explosion of East L.A. bands that arose in the wake of Valens's success and untimely death has been chronicled in several compilations. Varese Sarabande has released four volumes of *The West Coast East Side Sound*; the series was inspired by promoter–producer Eddie Davis's original late-'60s comps. Also worthy are Dionysus Records' *The East Side Sound* and the somewhat misleadingly titled *Pachuco Soul!* on the gray-market label Vampisoul. There is a good deal of track duplication among these sets. The most ambitious and handsome release is Minky Records' forthcoming *The Rampart Story*, a four-CD blockbuster surveying Eddie Davis's label ventures, with a handsome one-hundred-page book containing dozens of rare photos and notes by East L.A. writer (and Los Lobos familiar) Luis J. Rodriguez (*Always Running*) and veteran L.A. critic and discophile Don Waller.

Some East Side bands have had their individual albums reissued. The Premiers' *Farmer John Live* was rereleased by Collectors' Choice. Vampisoul has put out an expanded edition of Cannibal and the Headhunters' *Land of 1000 Dances* album. Minky issued a bulked-up CD version of the Mixtures' Linda album *Stompin' at the Rainbow*.

Thee Midniters, the most prolific of all East Side groups, receive comprehensive treatment on *Thee Complete Midniters* (Microwerks), which brings together their studio LPs on four CDs, augmented by bonus tracks (including the late-period singles "The Ballad of Cesar Chavez," in English and Spanish, and "Chicano Power"). If you're interested in nothing but the rockers, go for Norton Records' crunching *In Thee Midnite Hour!!!!* A mix of ballads and rockers can be found on Thump's *Thee Midniters Greatest*, with liner notes by yours truly. Lead singer Little Willie G.'s *Make Up for the Lost Time*, produced by David Hidalgo and released by HighTone in 2000, is a worthy comeback album that finds Willie Garcia's vocal chops undimmed by time.

Electric blues from the '60s played a big role in Los Lobos' work, and I would be remiss if I didn't recommend a few albums that definitely drove the band's early direction. *The Essential Otis Rush* (Fuel 2000) pulls together the southpaw Chicagoan's Cobra sides. Freddie King's complete studio work is spread over two enormous Bear Family boxed sets, *Taking Care of Business* and *Texas Flyer*, and I wouldn't be without a note of it; more economically inclined consumers are directed to *The Complete King–Federal Singles* (Real Gone), a two-CD overview of his most productive period. *Truckin' with Albert Collins* presents the best of the Texas guitarist's early singles, most of them instrumental. Someday an enterprising label will issue Jimmy Reed's collected oeuvre; until then, any edition of his two-LP Vee-Jay set *Jimmy Reed at Carnegie Hall*, not a live album but a terrific compilation of studio work, is probably the best bet.

The music of Captain Beefheart and His Magic Band cast a long shadow on the boundary-pushing music made by Los Lobos and the Latin Playboys in the '90s. Revenant's box *Grow Fins* offers a deep picture of Beefheart's transition from electric bluesman to left-field rock shaman. Good single-disc collections are *Safe as Milk* (1967, with Ry Cooder on slide guitar), the landmark *Trout Mask Replica* (1969, produced by Frank Zappa), and *The Mirror Man Sessions* (1999, containing out-of-this-world blues-based jams). Rhino's 2014 box *Sun Zoom Spark* compiles the Captain's terrific '70s albums issued under Warner's aegis.

English label Soul Jazz's *Chicano Power! Latin Rock in the USA, 1968–1976* is an overview of the funk-oriented Latino bands whose rise coincided with the political ferment of the era; though L.A. acts are in the minority here, the uncredited liner notes supply concise and worthwhile context. The seminal early-'70s East Side bands Tierra and El Chicano are represented on various greatest hits comps, all of them thinly annotated and disappointingly cheesy, but if you want the hits, like the former's "Together" or the latter's "Viva Tirado," they are there. A contemporaneous act worthy of attention is Oakland's multi-ethnic Tower of Power, whose fat funk sound inspired Cesar Rosas's pre-Lobos band Fast Company; the two-CD Rhino compilation *What Is Hip?* brings together the cream of the jazzy East Bay group's in-the-pocket recordings.

Jon Wilkman's 2009 PBS documentary *Chicano Rock! The Sounds of East Los Angeles,* narrated by Edward James Olmos, is an economical and informative history containing interviews with Los Lobos and a host of trend-setting East Side performers;

it is available on DVD from PBS Home Video. The Peabody Award–winning 2013 PBS series *Latino Americans* is available as a two-DVD set; it supplies background on the UFW, the East L.A. school walkouts, and the Chicano Moratorium of 1970.

Among Los Lobos' roots-oriented contemporaries on the L.A. punk scene of the '70s and '80s, the Blasters are the most important and influential. Their 1980 Rollin' Rock debut *American Music* was reissued in an expanded edition on CD and LP in 1997 by HighTone with new notes by this writer; all their Slash recordings, with bonus material, are on the two-CD Rhino set *Testament*, which is out of print but worth seeking out.

The punk–roots terrorist contingent is best represented by the Gun Club's *Fire of Love* and the Flesh Eaters' *A Minute to Pray, A Second to Die*, both of which were originally released by Slash Records' Ruby subsidiary and rereleased in 2014 by the Superior Viaduct label; the latter record features the "all-star" iteration of vocalist–lyricist Chris D.'s unit, with members of X, the Blasters, and, holding down the sax chair, Steve Berlin. Top Jimmy and the Rhythm Pigs' *Piggus Drunkus Maximus*, produced by Berlin and with liner notes by this writer, was issued on LP in 1987 by Down There, an indie label operated by Steve Wynn of L.A.'s Dream Syndicate; it has never been released on CD, but it is a terrific approximation of a Monday night at the Cathay de Grande in Hollywood.

The Knitters' joshing take on country and folk, with three members of X and the Blasters' Dave Alvin contributing, is best heard on their 1985 debut *Poor Little Critter in the Road* (Rhino). X's pre-rock roots are more felt than heard on their studio albums, all on CD via Rhino/Slash. If you want to hear John Doe and Exene sing Hank Williams, you can watch them do it in William T. Morgan's one-of-a-kind 1986 documentary *The Unheard Music* (MVD Visual DVD).

I wrote a personal summation of L.A.'s roots–punk epoch for Don Snowden's 1997 anthology *Make the Music Go Bang! The Early L.A. Punk Scene* (St. Martin's Griffin). The book, now out of print, is worth finding for its many evocative photographs by Gary Leonard, who scrupulously documented the scene.

Unfortunately unrepresented on CD and difficult to find outside the L.A. city limits (and even within them, for that matter) are the Plugz's self-released debut album *Electrify Me*, which contains the trio's revved-up "La Bamba," and Phast Phreddie and Thee Precisions' self-issued live album *West Hollywood Freeze-Out* and studio set *Limbo*.

Finally, two Los Lobos retrospectives, the two-CD *Just Another Band from East L.A.* (1993, and not to be confused with the group's like-titled 1978 acoustic album) and the four-CD box *El Cancionero Mas y Mas* (2000), both contain non-album tracks and rarities. The latter collection includes my notes about the band's history, from their chaotic 1980 debut at the Olympic Auditorium through the making of *This Time*.

Two East L.A. bands closely followed the trail cut by Los Lobos and ended up playing many of the same L.A. venues. The Blazers were a tight, eclectic quartet who cut four albums for Rounder Records; the first two, *Short Fuse* (1994) and *Eastside Soul* (1995), were produced by Cesar Rosas. The Delgado Brothers, three East Side *hermanos*, recorded a solid, bluesy set for HighTone Records, helmed by Robert Cray's producers Bruce Bromberg and Dennis Walker, in 1990.

Los Lobos' folk–rocking L.A. inheritors Quetzal and La Santa Cecilia themselves collected Grammy Awards in the Latin alternative category in consecutive years for, respectively, *Imaginaries* (2012) and *Trenta Dias* (2013). Mariachi El Bronx, the punk/*mariachi* fusion act that includes David Hidalgo's son Vincent among its members, issued a self-titled album on ATO Records in 2011. (Hidalgo's other son, David, Jr., drums for the long-running Southern California punk band Social Distortion.)